The MONOCLE
Travel Guide Series

30

Beirut

For more information,
please visit *gestalten.com*

Bibliographic information
published by the Deutsche
Nationalbibliothek: The Deutsche
Nationalbibliothek lists this
publication in the Deutsche
Nationalbibliografie; detailed
bibliographic data are available
online at *dnb.d-nb.de*

This book was printed on
paper certified by the FSC®

Monocle editor in chief
and chairman: *Tyler Brûlé*
Monocle editor: *Andrew Tuck*
Books editor: *Joe Pickard*
Guide editor: *Mikaela Aitken*

Designed by *Monocle*
Proofreading by *Monocle*
Typeset in *Plantin & Helvetica*

Printed by *Offsetdruckerei
Grammlich, Pliezhausen*

Made in Germany

Published by *Gestalten*, Berlin 2018
ISBN 978-3-89955-944-6

© Die Gestalten Verlag GmbH &
Co. KG, Berlin 2018

Welcome
—— Beirut
bounces back

Phoenix-like Beirut has been smashed by civil war (and war in general) but it's still arguably the greatest city in the Middle East – and certainly the most fun. It's *thrilling*, *beguiling* and *beautiful*, despite the religious faultlines and political fractures that run through it.

Historically it's the *ultimate enduring metropolis*, with a chronicle of Phoenician, Hellenistic, Roman, Byzantine, Arab, Crusader and Ottoman influences. Today it's bolstered by its large, ambitious and *loyal diaspora* and continues to reinvent, reconstruct and simply build – the latter a visible yet contentious presence.

There's a vibrant party life and rich food scene that ranges from neighbourhood cafés plating up Levantine favourites to smart new-wave restaurateurs making happy bedfellows of *tradition* and *modernity*. There's also a nurturing approach to *entrepreneurialism*, with art, design and fashion all taking a front seat in globalising the city's cultural output.

Though it may not have the infrastructure of, say, an efficient Swiss city, it remains doggedly *resilient*. It's a capital where the streets are crisscrossed with wires plugged audaciously into the electricity mains, where conventional addresses won't help you locate your hotel and where leaning on the horn of your Mercedes G-Wagon is urban therapy.

In many ways the city's character is seasoned and diversified by its hardships. Beirut's citizens have known real strife and they plan to dance, create, cook and pursue *la belle vie* while peace endures. Turn the page and join them. — (M)

Contents
—— Navigating the city

Use the key below to help navigate the guide section by section.

H Hotels

F Food and drink

R Retail

T Things we'd buy

E Essays

C Culture

D Design and architecture

S Sport and fitness

W Walks

O Out of town

Map
—— The city
at a glance

The motley collection of buildings scattered across the Lebanese capital is a visual representation of the city's history. The former Ottoman-style palaces in the east are a nod to the aristocratic 19th-century residents; the playful modernist and brutalist buildings in Ashrafieh and the beach clubs along the Corniche depict a frivolous chapter in the 1950s and 1960s; the pockmarked hotels in Hamra point to the 1975 to 1990 civil war; and the spangled developments in Downtown and Saifi Village reflect the city's contemporary ambitions.

Within this jumble you'll find dynamic communities that are creating colourful enclaves. On the outskirts to the west is the Armenian neighbourhood of Bourj Hammoud, while Gemmayzeh and Mar Mikhael are go-tos for restaurants, retail and late-night bars. Monot is a hot spot for well-heeled food fans, Clemenceau and Hamra are bulging with cultural stop-offs, Basta is packed with alluring antiques and Badaro is on the rise. The good news is that exploring on foot is achievable – minus those car-clogged arterials, of course.

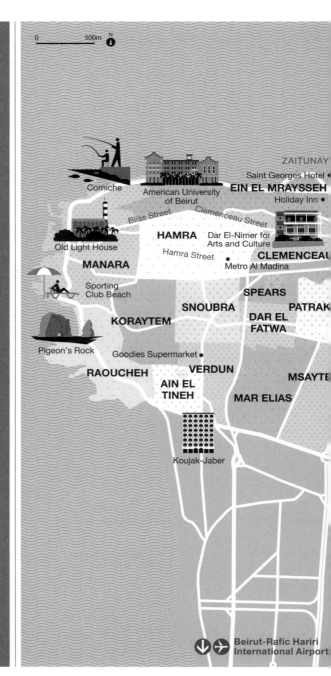

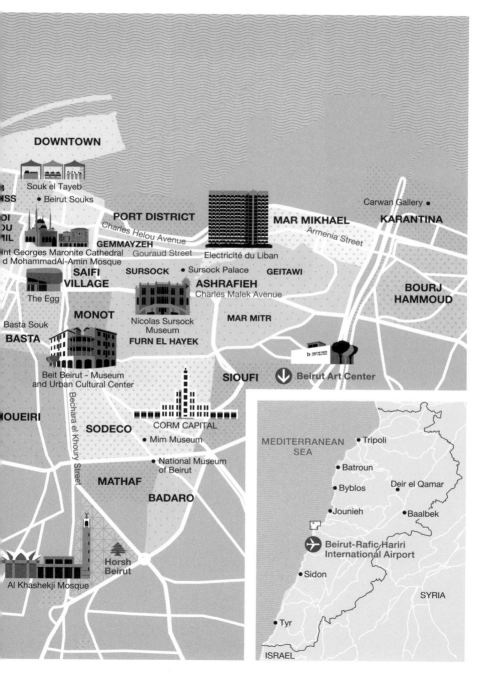

DOWNTOWN

Souk el Tayeb
● Beirut Souks

PORT DISTRICT
Charles Helou Avenue

Carwan Gallery ●

MAR MIKHAEL
Armenia Street

KARANTINA

GEMMAYZEH
Gouraud Street

int Georges Maronite Cathedral
d MohammadAl-Amin Mosque

Electricité du Liban

SAIFI
VILLAGE

SURSOCK
● Sursock Palace

GEITAWI

The Egg

ASHRAFIEH
Charles Malek Avenue

BOURJ
HAMMOUD

MONOT

Basta Souk

BASTA

Nicolas Sursock
Museum

FURN EL HAYEK

MAR MITR

Beit Beirut - Museum
and Urban Cultural Center

SIOUFI

b- ● Beirut Art Center

OUEIRI

Bechara el Khoury Street

CORM CAPITAL

SODECO

● Mim Museum

MEDITERRANEAN
SEA

● Tripoli

● National Museum
of Beirut

● Batroun

MATHAF

● Byblos

Deir el Qamar

BADARO

● Jounieh

● Baalbek

Beirut-Rafic Hariri
International Airport

Al Khashekji Mosque

Horsh
Beirut

● Sidon

SYRIA

● Tyr

ISRAEL

Need to know
—— Get to grips with the basics

Navigating the city
Route finders

Prior to street names being introduced in the 1940s, Beirut's neighbourhoods were differentiated depending on who called them home or which landmarks were present. Formal names were assigned after independence but they're rarely visible and haven't become part of the navigational vernacular.

Instead, landmarks are still key to getting around and there's an informal hierarchical system used to navigate you first to the general area and then to the exact spot. In the initial tier are government buildings, foreign embassies and religious sites; next come hospitals and universities; then banks, petrol stations and shops; and finally billboards, building sites and local characters (a popular one in Gemmayzeh was a plump pooch). It seems overwhelming but once you're thrown into the throng it'll make sense.

In this guide we've provided street names where possible but building names and landmarks will likely prove more useful. Pick up a free Zawarib map in town. This Beirut-based company has noted all the landmarks that locals will invariably direct you to.

Money matters
Cashing in

Everywhere accepts both the Lebanese lira (also referred to as the Lebanese pound) and US dollars; when paying by card or withdrawing cash, you can choose which currency to use. There's no standard for tipping and it varies as to whether gratuity is included in a bill. Therefore if you've received good service, it's polite to leave a 15 per cent tip – except in taxis, where paying extra is uncommon.

Spelling bee
No wrong answers

Neighbourhoods, streets, landmarks and shops have various iterations of spelling in English. This quirk is due to the phonetic nature of translating Arabic letters to fit within the English alphabet. The split in the public-schooling system between French and English schools is also a factor. When translating Arabic names there are English and French approaches to spelling: Ashrafieh and Achrafieh, or Zokak el Blat and Zuqaq al Blat. In this frenetic city the inconsistency of spelling is one of the only constants.

You make it look so easy!

The changing skyline
Money talks

In 1994, the late prime minister Rafik Hariri created a share-holding corporation with property-owners and investors to turn the bombed city centre into a showcase for Lebanon. This company, Solidere, is a public-private hybrid that benefits from both regulatory authority and being listed on the Beirut Stock Exchange.

Its renewal of more than 200 hectares of central Beirut has called on top architects such as Jean Nouvel, Sir Norman Foster and Zaha Hadid. However, progress has been met with opposition from locals who feel that the essence of the more than 4,000-year-old city is being destroyed in favour of international investment, luxury retailers and high-rises.

Belle vie
Thrills and spills

Putting Beirut's enduring clichés aside, you would be hard-pressed to find any other Middle Eastern city bearing graffiti by the Arab Lesbian Liberation Front. And there are few places where you can tuck into organic tabbouleh while army tanks rumble past.

Beirut isn't about world-leading urbanism, green architecture or great public transport. Yet for all its contradictions it's a great place to live and a thrilling city to visit, with a palpable sense of freedom, a vibrant creative community and an unabashed will to live la belle vie, no matter what. So embrace the long business lunches, weeknight revelry and endless stream of club nights and launch parties.

Superior hospitality
Home away from home

Although the nomadic custom of looking after strangers seeking shelter is no longer necessary, life in the Arabic-speaking world still revolves around accommodating guests in every way possible. Nothing exemplifies this better than the commonly heard refrain "*ahlan wa sahlan*", which means "welcome" but can be translated as, "you're among family, be at ease".

People here share what they have without expecting anything in return, merely trusting that if one day they called on you, you would return the kindness. So don't be alarmed when a shopkeeper offers you a cup of coffee – sit awhile and soak up the unwavering hospitality.

Resilient residents
Forging forward

Lebanon is no stranger to instability. The past few decades alone have seen civil war, the 2005 assassination of then prime minister Rafik Hariri, the 2006 Israeli conflict, the beginning of the garbage crisis and subsequent protests in 2015, the Syrian war that at times has spilled over into Lebanon and, more recently, the refugee crisis.

However, the resilient country welcomed 1.7 million tourists in 2016 – not bad for a country of six million people. Time and again, Lebanon and its capital have fostered hospitality, snappy entrepreneurialism and layered cultural, retail and dining offerings – something that feels habitual even if the political climate falters.

Viticulture
Grape heights

Lebanon had five wineries in 1988 but now has almost 50 that produce about eight million bottles of wine a year – no mean feat for an industry suffering from lacklustre government support. Increasingly, makers are experimenting with both native and imported grapes.

The Bekaa Valley, sandwiched between Mount Lebanon and the Syrian border, is the most prominent wine region with crops protected by cool summer nights, while Mount Lebanon and Batroun both benefit from exposure to the Mediterranean. Up-and-coming labels are also popping up in the microclimates of the valleys and plateaus in the far south.

Getting around town
Servees!

The advent of taxi apps are making navigation in Beirut's tangled streets a little less daunting for first-time visitors. But the drivers tend to rely on the apps' maps, which will often send them in the wrong direction.

To combat this, flag down a *servees* – you'll know it by its red number plate. Shout your destination (or the closest landmark) to the driver and don't be discouraged if the first few turn you down: existing customers are likely heading in another direction. Once approved, negotiate your price – basic journeys should cost no more than LBP3,000 a person. If this all feels too adventurous, ask your hotel or a restaurant to phone a trusted cab company for you.

Cor blimey, that was close…

Our top picks:

01 **Papercup:** The place to enjoy a smooth latte and browse some top titles.
see page 60

02 **Interdesign Showroom:** Check out the quirks of this raw-concrete tower.
see page 106

03 **National Museum of Beirut:** Soak up the city's ancient past to better understand its present.
see page 85

04 **Plan Bey:** Come here for colourful souvenirs.
see page 55

05 **Tawlet:** One of our favourite spots for a low-key but delectable lunch.
see pages 27

06 **Holiday Inn:** This brutalist war relic is worth a visit.
see page 113

07 **Issam Fares Institute:** Admire Zaha Hadid's otherworldly structure.
see pages 118

08 **Mim Museum:** Fancy marvelling at some jaw-dropping minerals?
see page 87

09 **Beirut Art Center:** Expand your artistic horizons here.
see page 89

10 **Sporting Club:** The perfect place to cool off with a cocktail by the sea.
see page 122

Hotels
—— Make
yourself at home

Two extremes rule the roost when it comes to Beirut's best lodging options: quaint guesthouses, often run out of restored Ottoman palaces or early 20th-century family homes, and indulgent five-star luxury chains that operate like well-oiled machines. We've put together a list of worthy contenders from both categories, plus a few of the outliers that break the city's expected moulds through their outlandish eclecticism.

In addition, since each neighbourhood is infinitely different in temperament – and therefore what it offers – we've included a healthy geographical spread to help you explore the city's many areas. Regardless of location, however, one thing remains constant across all options: the sheer cordiality of Lebanese hospitality.

1

Baffa House, Mar Mikhael
Family affair

"The way to get to know a country is to meet its people," says Orphée Haddad, founder of L'Hote Libanais (The Lebanese Host). The guesthouse collective has four Beirut locations, including Dar al Achrafieh (*opposite*) and Baffa House.

Samer Ghorayeb's family home, which he opened in 2014, is located in a Bauhaus-style building. The high-ceilinged spaces include one twin and three double rooms, a communal lounge and a dining area where the full Lebanese breakfast spread is served each morning – complete with jams courtesy of Ghorayeb's mother. All rooms feature carefully restored vintage furniture that he has salvaged from soon-to-be-demolished palaces and old apartment blocks.
Patriarch Arida Street
+961 81 668 221
baffahouse.com

MONOCLE COMMENT: In the lounge are family photos, playful artworks by Ghorayeb's aunt Laure and 1960s sketchings by his father's architecture students.

② Dar al Achrafieh,
Furn el Hayek
Personal touch

Lovers of Lebanese nostalgia
should head to the two-
bedroom Dar al Achrafieh,
which Jamil Azar (*pictured*)
opened in 2005 on the third
floor of a 1920s building. The
flat was added to the building
by Azar's parents in 1953 and
is full of the family's mid-
century furniture.

"I want to show guests that
there's more to Lebanon than
they've been told," says Azar,
who has lived here his whole
life and is always on hand. He
aims to give people a personal
experience that they couldn't
get in big hotels. "At breakfast
we sit together. It's as if they
belong to our family while
they're here."
Salim Bustros
+961 (0)1 217 006
hotelibanais.com

Don't
mind me

④
Beit el Tawlet, Mar Mikhael
Dynamic duo

Food campaigner and writer
Kamal Mouzawak (*see page
74*) and womenswear designer
Rabih Kayrouz (*see page 59*)
are behind one of Beirut's
newest guesthouses. Opened in
2018, Beit el Tawlet sits above
Mouzawak's restaurant of the
same name (*see page 27*). This
is the fourth guesthouse from
the formidable duo but their
first in the capital.

The rooms are comfortable
and relaxed, with every detail
considered. "It's like you're living
in our house," says Mouzawak.
The decor feels 1970s (in a
good way), with rattan furniture,
plenty of greenery, playful
lampshades and Rana Salam
artworks (*see page 51*).
Chalhoub Building 22,
12 Nahr Street
+961 (0)1 448 129
beiteltawlet.com

③
Four Seasons Hotel Beirut,
Downtown
Opulent option

The benefit of booking a
room in a dependable chain
is the reliable quality and
Four Seasons' Beirut outpost
is a case in point. From high
tea in the lobby to sushi and
cocktails at the rooftop bar,
the 230-room hotel is dripping
with decadence.

The cabinets are stocked
with the country's finest
wines, the kitchens are run by
exceptional chefs – including
an in-house baker turning
out fresh *manoushe* (herby
flatbread) – and the spa
features the nimblest of fingers.
1418 Professor Wafic Sinno Avenue
+961 (0)1 761 000
fourseasons.com/beirut

Catch you at the Corniche!

MONOCLE COMMENT: This is
no low-key affair, as evident
from the soaring tower and its
proximity to the Solidere-built
Zaitunay Bay luxury-yacht
marina. The vistas from the
decks of the pool on the 26th
floor are also super.

⑤
Villa Clara, Mar Mikhael
Works a charm

When it comes to the spirited warmth of Lebanese hospitality, Villa Clara is hard to beat. Husband-and-wife owners Olivier Gougeon and Marie-Hélène Moawad run a relaxed and welcoming guesthouse staffed by a bright and attentive team.

All seven rooms and shared foyers are packed to the rafters with artworks by the likes of Tagreed Darghouth, Sabhan Adam and Marwan Sahmarani, plus pieces of furniture by Mondrian, Nada Debs and even antique chairs from the French senate. Collecting is Moawad's passion, cooking Gougeon's. By the age of 25 he was a pastry chef in Paris's three Michelin-starred restaurant Le Grand Véfour so naturally the French-cross-Mediterranean fare is cracking.
Rue Khenchara
+961 70 995 739
villaclara.fr

MONOCLE COMMENT: It's easy to while away an entire day within Villa Clara's walls. But Moawad and Gougeon may well chivvy you out the door with a list of their favourite haunts.

Al Bustan Hotel, Beit Mery

Granted, this cheery hotel on the hilltop overlooking the city isn't technically in Beirut but it's only a half-hour drive up the hill to Beit Mery if the city becomes too stifling. The air is noticeably cooler up here and the pace of life beneath the towering pines is mellow – an atmosphere that founder Emile Bustani wanted to capture when he drafted plans to build a hotel for his friends and colleagues back in 1962.

The striking mid-century flair extends from the white-and-carmine balconies to the wood-panelled telephone booths in reception and the concierge's teal jacket. The hotel is now in the hands of the third generation – Laura Lahoud has maintained its original charm while updating rooms to fend off staidness. Lahoud and her mother have also cloaked the walls with an expanding art collection and created a following for their annual performing-arts festival held in the hotel's purpose-built 450-seat auditorium every February and March.
hotelalbustan.com

⑥
The Albergo, Monot
Confluence of influences

Initially this stop-in may seem frenetic: its rooms, reception and restaurants are all decorated differently and crammed with oddities. But after a fortified pink lemonade it's hard not to appreciate the frantic genius of Lebanese-born, London-based designer Tarfa Salam. "Lebanon was ruled by the Ottomans and the French but also had Italian influences; we've translated this in the decor," says general manager Jihane Khairallah. "We don't want to rival other hotels in town."

The hotel is opening a twin building next door, increasing the 33 rooms to more than 50. The offering will also include four restaurants (including, according to the hotel, Beirut's first Italian restaurant, which opened in 1992), a gym, spa, hamam and rooftop pool.
137 Rue Abdel Wahab El Inglizi
+961 (0)1 339 797
albergobeirut.com

MONOCLE COMMENT: Two of the many draw cards here include outdoor breakfasts on the roof terrace and a bartender who won't retire for the night until you're ready to do the same.

⑦

Hayete, Furn el Hayek
Small but perfectly formed

Towards the northern edge of Ashrafieh is a gem of a boutique hotel called Hayete. The four-bedroom guesthouse in a heritage-listed 1920s residential building is run by brother and sister Elias and Caroline Rahban.

The cheery space is playfully kitted out, with vintage furniture and artwork salvaged from flea markets, as well as mouth-blown glass lamps and hand-woven cotton towels, both from Syria. The East and North rooms are ensuites while the West and South benefit from private balconies. Breakfast is prepared fresh for each guest until as late as 14.30 and includes *manoushe* from the neighbourhood's namesake Furn el Hayek bakery.
1F, Masabni Building, Shukri Al Asli Street
+961 70 239 912
hayete-guesthouse.com

MONOCLE COMMENT: Hosts Elias and Caroline are always happy to share their insight on Beirut over a beer on the balcony. They can also arrange private drivers for day trips to the mountains or coastal towns.

Hotels hounded by war

01 Le Bristol, Snoubra: This hotel opened in 1951 and played host to crisis talks and peace negotiations between Lebanon's warring political factions during the 1975 to 1990 civil war. It received a complete facelift in 2015.
lebristolbeirut.com

02 The Mayflower, Hamra: The wood-panelled Duke of Wellington bar, which was a favoured watering hole for foreign correspondents during the civil war, is still open and continues to serve stiff drinks.
mayflowerbeirut.com

03 Saint George Hotel, Ein el Mraysseh: The Saint-George was devastated in the civil war. The owner began restoration but was halted by legislation over the government-backed Solidere rebuild of Downtown. During this standoff a car bomb killed then prime minister Rafik Hariri outside the hotel in 2005. It has remained in ruins ever since.
saintgeorgebeirut.com

04 Holiday Inn, Ein el Mraysseh: Snipers used to base themselves in this now-hollow shell (*see page 113*). It still stands, pockmarked with bullet and artillery holes, and acts as a car park for military tanks.

05 Le Commodore Hotel, Hamra: Another haunt of foreign journalists who covered the Israeli invasion and Lebanon's civil war. It had a facelift in 2004, ahead of its 50th anniversary in 2008. Sadly, the News Bar is now The Lounge.
lecommodorehotel.com

8
Phoenicia Hotel, Ein el Mraysseh
Restored to former glories

When the Phoenicia first opened during Lebanon's golden days in 1961, its mid-century terraced balconies and extravagant restaurant and pool were beacons of swinging frivolity. However, like the Holiday Inn to its rear and Saint George Hotel out front, the luxury lodging fell into ruin during the civil war.

Fortunately the Phoenicia bounced back and reopened in 2000 with 446 rooms and suites, as well as 33 apartments and a penthouse, all spread across three towers. The former opulence reigns supreme in both the rooms and the chandelier-spangled marble lobby. The hotel also hosts satellite shopfronts for Aïshti, Rodeo Drive and Iwan Maktabi.
Minet el Hosn
+961 (0)1 369 100
phoeniciabeirut.com

MONOCLE COMMENT: West-facing balcony rooms in the original tower are positioned to enjoy a vista overlooking the impressive pool scene below, as well as the lively Corniche beyond.

⑨
O Monot Hotel, Monot
Taking care of business

This smallish stopover caters to Beirut's relative absence of business hotels. The independent 41-room affair is locally owned and managed under the banner of London-based Small Luxury Hotels.

It's located within walking distance of both the upmarket bars and restaurants of Monot and the growing business district around the Beirut Souks. Interior architect Claude Missir outfitted the interiors with a clean and modern look and the rooftop bar and plunge pool overlook The Egg (*see page 112*) and Mohammad al-Amin Mosque (*see page 115*).
Monot Street
+961 (0)1 338 777
omonot.com

MONOCLE COMMENT: Killing time between meetings? Play a game of chess on the owner's antique board with bronze and silver pieces. You'll find it in a quiet back corner of the lobby.

Come and join me, why don't you?

⑩
Le Gray, Downtown
Boutique but luxurious

All it took was one trip to Beirut for hotelier Gordon Campbell Gray to decide to open an outpost here. Founded in 2009, with a costly expansion designed by Lebanese architect Galal Mahmoud in 2017, the luxury hotel operates more as a boutique offering compared to the larger international chains present in the city.

Located in the thick of the Downtown crush, its 103 rooms overlook sights such as the Roman ruins and the Beirut Souks. Having said that, you'll find the best perch by the infinity pool on the roof, where the decks turn into a bar as night falls.
Martyrs' Square
+961 (0)1 971 111
campbellgrayhotels.com/
le-gray-beirut

MONOCLE COMMENT: The colours of some of the soft furnishings may be a little brash but the walnut *Musharabia* (wooden latticework) on the ceilings of the suites by British interior designer Mary Fox Linton tie the rooms nicely into the city and its surrounds.

Food and drink
—— A Middle Eastern feast

One of the major draws of a trip to Lebanon is the food – and rightly so. The following pages will take you well beyond the tabbouleh and hummus that you'll find at home and into a world teeming with cherry-drenched kebabs and yoghurt spiked with tahini.

The Arabic food in Beirut is Levantine – encompassing not just Lebanese but also Armenian, Syrian and Palestinian influences – and it's more diverse and infinitely richer than you might expect. Thanks to its Med-side location you will also find a fantastic spread of seafood and southern European specialities, from which we've picked our favourites – whether French fine-dining or Neapolitan street pizza. *Sahtein*!

Levantine restaurants
Regional fare

①
Liza, Furn el Hayek
Popular classic

The Lebanese outpost of Liza and Ziad Asseily's Paris restaurant sprawls over the first floor of an Ottoman house in the heart of Ashrafieh. Interior designer Maria Ousseimi's flair is felt throughout, with details that include wallpaper evoking south Lebanon's banana fields and locally made Bokja furniture (*see page 52*).

The food is classic Arabic with a twist: think *fatteh batinjen* with basil, a herby take on the yoghurt-and-aubergine dish. Be sure to book.
*Metropolitan Club,
Doumani Street*
+961 (0)1 208 108
lizabeirut.com

Just a small pre-dinner snack...

2 Café Em Nazih, Gemmayzeh
Much-loved hangout

A large, airy space filled with
hanging plants and long
wooden tables, Café Em Nazih
is never empty – and with
good reason. Everyone from
solo travellers to large birthday
groups flock here at all times
of day for its reasonably priced
and consistently excellent
Lebanese mezze and daily
dishes (the *kibbeh laban*, meat-
filled bulgur torpedos in warm
yoghurt, are particularly good).

Arabic music is the order
of the day and the live acts at
the weekends are so popular
that you'll need to reserve in
advance. The rest of the time
just drop by and enjoy the
good vibes. There's also a
great pub quiz on Wednesdays.
Saifi Urban Gardens,
Pasteur Street
+961 (0)1 562 509
saifigardens.com/en/cafe

Must-try
Lahmadjun from Ichkhanian
Bakery, Zokak el Blat
This family-owned bakery
has been perfecting its tiny
menu since 1946. Its Armenian
version of this thin, meat-
topped pizza is unrivalled
come breakfast; there's also
a vegetarian option. Note: it's
closed on Mondays.
+961 (0)1 375 178

③
Em Sherif, Monot
The full monty

Yes, the decadent hand-painted
ceilings and mirrored tables
are a lot to take in. But hang
in there because if you can get
used to the extravagant interior
an onslaught (33 dishes to be
exact) of truly exceptional food
awaits you.

This is a set-menu affair so
pace yourself and leave room
for a taste of each regional
dish assembled by the chef
and co-owner, Mireille Hayek.
Expect outstanding basics
such as hummus and *muttabal*,
pastries from the in-house
bakery, succulent grilled
chicken and beef, plus six
different traditional desserts.
From the crowd to the live
Arabic music, this is Lebanon
at its flamboyant best.
Victor Hugo Street
+961 (0)1 206 206
emsherif.com

④

Tawlet, Mar Mikhael
Regional tour de force

Set up by social entrepreneur
Kamal Mouzawak, Tawlet
("table") embodies the best
of Lebanese food culture:
real hospitality, a relaxed
atmosphere and delicious food.
Classics such as tabbouleh
are cooked by a mixture of
in-house and guest chefs, and
served buffet-style along with
lesser-known regional dishes
that you'd be hard pressed to
find elsewhere in Beirut.

The lunch-only menu
changes daily according to the
cook's hometown, with Syrian,
Armenian and Palestinian
dishes appearing regularly. The
long wooden tables are ideal
for enjoying an afternoon with
a bottle of Lebanese wine.
12 Naher Street,
off Armenia Street
+961 (0)1 448 129
soukeltayeb.com/tawlet

⑤

Mezyan, Hamra
Boogie nights

A cornerstone of the food-
and-drink scene in Hamra,
airy and inviting Mezyan
has acquired cult-like status in
Beirut, becoming a day-and-
night favourite for the city's
intelligentsia. The reasonably
priced menu boasts a vast
variety of Middle Eastern
dishes, from chicken liver
with pomegranate molasses
to lamb tagine with prunes
and almonds, alongside
Mediterranean bites such
as calamari.

Come nightfall, Beirutis
descend on Mezyan to dance
the night away to Arabic tunes.
There's often live music and
usually some raucous *dabke*,
a traditional Levantine jig.
Rasamny Building,
Hamra Street
+961 (0)1 740 608

Taking stock
——
A food shop that sells mainly
snacks and booze, Hibou's
24/7 delivery service has made
it a key part of many Beirutis'
lives. As a result, no party ever
needs to run dry and late-night
hunger pangs are easily salved.
+961 (0)1 339 306

⑦

Enab, Mar Mikhael
Auntie's favourite

From the mismatched cemento tiles and the rambling garden to the pastel-coloured, trinket-adorned interior, this is the kind of place that reminds you of an eccentric grandmother's home. Thankfully, the food also meets the standards of any Lebanese *teta* – and that's high praise in Beirut.

On top of the usual mezze plates you can also get some lesser-known dishes, including marinated frogs. The large outdoor area is perfect on sticky summer nights.
Geara Building, Armenia Street
+961 (0)1 444 441

6

Abdel Wahab, Monot
Nostalgia trip

Named after the street on which it sits, Abdel Wahab became a landmark in upscale Ashrafieh not long after it opened in 1999. Co-owner Jean-Claude Ghosn says the idea was to create "a traditional neighbourhood spot" and it's fair to say that he's succeeded.

The mezze is good (not quite excellent) but it's the lively and typically Lebanese atmosphere that's the biggest draw. That, along with the summertime terrace, is a strong pull for locals – the restaurant is busy most evenings. Water fountains, bubbling shisha pipes and the scent of arak make for an evocative evening that appeals to all the senses.
51 Abdel Wahab el Inglizi Street
+961 (0)1 200 550

Must-try
Shawarma wrap from Barbar, Hamra
Slivers of chicken, pickles, chips and garlicky *toum* sauce, all tightly wrapped in flatbread. It's open all day but no visit to Beirut is complete without a late-night stop at this fast-food institution – *the* place for a midnight feast.
+961 (0)1 753 330

⑨ Abou Hassan, Bourj Hammoud
No-frills perfection

Located in the heart of Armenian neighbourhood Bourj Hammoud, Abou Hassan may be off the beaten track but it's oh so worth seeking out. Open day and night, it's always full, whether with families enjoying breakfast or tipsy friends satisfying some late-night munchies.

This is the place to savour Arabic staples (using your fingers and hot, fresh bread): *fatteh*, chickpeas and fried bread in garlicky yoghurt; *foul*, lemony stewed fava beans; and, of course, hummus and its chickpea-heavy relatives *balila* and *msabaha*. Plus a giant plate of pickled vegetables. Still hungry? Try the fried egg with meat – rich and flavourful.
Mar Youssef Street
+961 (0)1 266 888

⑧ T-marbouta, Hamra
Mezze maestro

Known for its activist crowd and generous portions of lip-smackingly good Levantine food, this is a great option for feasting on a budget. Highlights include the spicy potatoes, lentil kibbeh and the juicy Aleppan kebab, all of which are best enjoyed in the garden, with its coloured window shutters and plant-covered walls.

As well as being a fine place to get away from the noise and heat of the city, T-marbouta also features a library and regularly hosts cultural events.
Hamra Street
+961 (0)1 350 274
t-marbouta.com

⑩ Almayass, Furn el Hayek
Armenian indulgence

Established in 1996, Almayass was originally a place for the Alexandrian family to share their take on Levantine-Armenian food, a cuisine developed in exile after the Armenian genocide. What began as a family-run business has grown into a high-end worldwide franchise, yet the timeless original branch in the heart of leafy Ashrafieh still exudes warmth and intimacy.

Don't miss the *manti* – tiny, crispy meat dumplings in a creamy yoghurt sauce – or the kebab *karaz*: melt-in-the-mouth beef drizzled with a tart cherry dressing made specially by Armenians in the Lebanese city of Anjar.
Trabaud Street
+961 (0)1 215 046
almayass.com

Sheesh! That's good

Help yourself

Every Friday, Ashghalouna serves a tasty lunch buffet of home-style Lebanese food in the garden of an old Ottoman palace, now home to a charity that helps widows and orphans. After lunch, browse the boutique of handmade goods. Reservations recommended.
+961 (0)1 366 758

⑪
Maryool, Mar Mikhael
Share nicely

A collaboration between
restaurateur Karim Arakji –
also behind Meat the Fish
(*see page 37*) – and former
Tawlet (*see page 27*) chef
Reem Azoury, this small sun-
drenched restaurant offers a
little bit of everything.

From hearty home cooking
to unusual small plates and dips
inspired by Iraq, Yemen, Iran
and elsewhere, everything is
made for sharing; the *musakhan*
taco, which is a modern update
on a Palestinian chicken-and-
sumac classic, is unmissable.
Meanwhile, the interior is
minimal but pretty. Beiruti
architecture firm Ghaith & Jad
used Italian terrazzo tiles for
the walls, benches and floor
to wonderful effect.
Pharaon Street
+961 (0)1 442 045
maryool.com

⑫
Seza, Mar Mikhael
Romantic retreat

Tucked away in the corner
plot of a quiet backstreet
in Mar Mikhael, this tiny,
romantic Armenian restaurant
oozes unassuming charm.
From the friendly waiters to
the top-notch food and the
complimentary Arabic desserts,
Seza gets it right from start
to finish.

For newcomers to Armenian
cuisine, try the set menu.
Staff deliver several tables'
worth of classics, including
muhammara (a spicy paste
of roasted red peppers and
walnuts) and *itch* (a tomatoey
take on tabbouleh). Wash it
all down with as many glasses
of aniseed-flavoured arak
as you can handle. The best
seats in the house are on the
leafy terrace.
Patriarch Arida Street
+961 (0)1 570 711

⑬

Al Falamanki, Raouche
Room with a view

Chintzy furnishings aside, there's a lot to love about the second branch of Al Falamanki: think Fairouz's dulcet tones drifting on the sea breeze, a view of Pigeon's Rock and dishes of exceptional Lebanese, Syrian and Armenian food.

Open from 09.00 to 02.00, the kitchen serves everything from a breakfast of *saj* flatbread, cheese and baked egg to lunch of stuffed Aleppan kibbeh and cherry kofta. Perched on the edge of a cliff, the views are phenomenal – especially at sunset. But the atmosphere is inviting at all times, including late in the evening when shisha and backgammon are the name of the game.
Charles de Gaulle Street
+961 (0)1 808 011
alfalamanki.com

Wineries to watch

01 Chateau Ksara, Bekaa Valley: The oldest and largest winery in Lebanon. Try the Cuvée du Troisième Millénaire or Le Souverain for a deep-bodied red with hints of berries.
chateauksara.com

02 Ixsir, Batroun: Although based up north in the mountains, most of Ixsir's grapes are actually grown in the more hospitable Bekaa Valley. The zippy Altitudes white is perfect for summer nights.
ixsir.com

03 Massaya, Bekaa Valley: Look out for the Terrasses de Baalbeck, a medium-depth red made of grapes grown near the city of Baalbek, fittingly the site of the Roman Bacchus Temple.
massaya.com

04 Domaine Wardy, Bekaa Valley: Having originally produced arak, the Wardy family have shifted their focus to wine. Try the fruity Obeideh, made from a native white grape previously reserved for the aniseed liqueur.
domainewardy.com

05 Karam Wines, Jezzine: The pioneering Karam brothers were the first to plant wine grapes in the south of Lebanon. The Saint John and the Maison are two reds of note.
karamwines.com

06 Chateau Musar, Keserwan: Probably the best known of Lebanon's wineries internationally, most of Musar's grapes are grown in the Bekaa Valley. The Hochar Père et Fils is a delicious red with layers of fruit and spice.
chateaumusar.com

International restaurants
Worldly cuisine

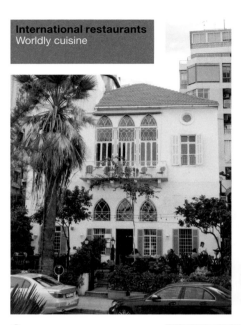

1

Casablanca, Ein el Mraysseh
Beside the sea

When designer Johnny Farah
and his Chinese wife Cyn
opened Casablanca in 1997,
it was the first restaurant to
return to a previously buzzing
area destroyed by the 1975 to
1990 civil war. Two decades
on, the place is an institution,
with many key staff and menu
items unchanged.

The food is eclectic: think
handmade prawn gyoza or
black Angus beef with wasabi.
"It's the kind of thing we eat
at home," says Farah. Located
in a colourfully renovated
old Lebanese house with
marvellous sea views, this is
a popular spot for lunch and
dinner, as well as the famous
weekend brunch. Don't miss
the saké list.
*Qaddoura Building,
Dar al-Mreisseh Street*
+961 (0)1 369 334

*Look no
further
for your
fresh fish*

②
Makan, Mar Mikhael
Ever-changing foods

Whether you dine inside
among the carefully chosen
prints or outside in the serene
bamboo-fringed garden,
Makan has the feel of a sun-
dappled Mediterranean
pied-à-terre. Given that it's
run by the people behind Plan
Bey (*see page 55*), Zawal (*see
page 48*) and Beyt Amir, the
clear vision is no surprise.
    Lunchtime revolves
around achingly good
Lebanese and Sri Lankan
food, a surprising combination
that chef Nimal Wasantha
knocks out of the park. Dinner
changes every three nights
according to the resident chef
at the time. You can expect
anything from Thai to Italian,
always beautifully presented.
Patriarch Arida Street
+96 (0)1 7095 4057
mottorestaurant.wordpress.com

③
Mitsu-ya, Gemmayzeh
Authentic touch

Located among Gouraud
Street's intimate bars, Mitsu-ya
has managed to distinguish
itself from the many other
popular Japanese spots in the
capital by providing a truly
authentic experience. The
unpretentious restaurant is
run by chef Mitsu Arai, who
has compiled a menu that
covers classic sushi, sashimi
and tempura, and also
experiments with inventive
cold and hot dishes.
    The best seats in the house
are at the bar, beneath the
traditional lanterns hanging
from the ceiling. Order an
Omakase ("I'll leave it up to
you") meal paired with saké
and wait for Arai to serve
whatever is freshest and most
delicious that day.
Gouraud Street
+961 (0)1 561 110

5

Couqley, Gemmayzeh
French flair

Walk down a tiny alleyway off busy Gouraud Street and you'll find an unexpected slice of Paris. Without straying into the naff, Couqley manages to capture the spirit of a brasserie with its chequered cloths, terrace tables and carafes of French wine.

Head chef and co-owner Alexis Couquelet learned his trade in the French capital – and it shows. The star dish is steak frites with Sauce Couqley; though that said, the onion soup and steak tartare deserve a mention.
The Alleyway, Gouraud Street
+961 (0)1 442 678
couqley.com

4

Eat Sunshine, Monot
Healthy goodness

Look no further than Eat Sunshine to satisfy all your superfood needs. This little conservatory-style café boasts an extensive breakfast and lunch-only menu to meet every dietary requirement, ranging from açai bowls and buckwheat pancakes to gluten-free bread.

Nearly all the ingredients are organic and locally sourced, with owner Dalia Taher aiming for food that's "healthy but tastes as good as the real thing". The portions are generous, the staff knowledgeable and the place is set in a lovely hidden-away courtyard overlooked by trees – cool in the summer and cosy in the winter.
Monot Street
+961 (0)1 325 980
eatsunshine.com

6
Baron, Mar Mikhael
Understated brilliance

Athanasios Kargatzidis'
plan was to move to Canada.
Then he saw this space and,
by 2016, Baron had opened
its doors. Whether it's the
industrial interior by Far
Architects or the line-up of
Mediterranean dishes that
linger in the mind, Baron has
become a food fixture on Mar
Mikhael's temperamental
restaurant scene.

Hospitality veteran
Kargatzidis is in the kitchen
most days, supervising a
rotating menu that creatively
marries regional ingredients
such as pomegranate molasses
and dukkah spice mix with
more European elements,
including pork sausages and
wood-barrelled feta.
Building 125, Pharaon Street
+961 (0)1 565 199
baronbeirut.com

⑦
Burgundy, Saifi Village
It's all in the name

Fuelled by their mutual love
of Burgundy in France, Ziad
Mouawad and Edmond Asseily
decided to open a restaurant
in Beirut with an expansive
impressive French wine menu.

Chef Youssef Akiki, who
trained alongside fêted French
chef Joël Robuchon, uses
locally sourced produce for
his dynamic seasonal menu.
The truffle tartines, *hamachi*
carpaccio and marinated
tuna on rice soufflé are just
a few of the dishes that keep
locals coming back, despite
the steep price tags.
752 Gouraud Street
+961 (0)1 999 820
burgundybeirut.com

⑧
Jaï, Clemenceau
Good things, small packages

There may only be one tiny table inside a room so small that the kitchen and restaurant are basically one but don't be fooled by Jaï's size – this place packs a punch. The hard-working chefs churn out fresh and tasty food from across south and east Asia, whether you're in the mood for onion bhajis and nasi goreng or fish cakes and laksa noodle soup.

It's located on a quiet street in Clemenceau and you can easily pull up a stool for a quick bite. Or order to-go, and enjoy it down on the Corniche.
Mexico Street
+961 (0)1 341 940
jai.kitchen

⑨
Lux, Port District
Cruise of the Med

Tucked away in an oft-ignored corner of Beirut, Lux feels like something of a hidden gem. The food is by Johnny Farah of Casablanca fame (*see page 32*) and the seasonal cocktails come courtesy of Michel Saidah, owner of Pacifico, one of the oldest bars in Beirut.

The fare is Mediterranean in the truest sense – with plates ranging from Greek grilled octopus to Gazan fish tagine – and most of the herbs and vegetables come straight from the owners' organic farm in the Chouf mountains. On Friday nights a DJ takes to the decks and the place is rammed with a who's-who of Beirut's bubbling creative scene.
El Jamarek/Darwish Haddad
+961 (0)1 444 311

⑩
La Pizzaria, Gemmayzeh
Straight from Napoli

Owner Fady Abounaoum doesn't do things by halves. Before opening La Pizzaria in 2015 he spent a year in Napoli learning how to make the perfect pizza and then another year training his staff.

Nearly all of his ingredients are imported from Italy: San Daniele prosciutto, Neapolitan mozzarella, San Marzano tomato sauce – even his wood-fired oven is Italian-built. The petite nature of the place, with tables spilling out onto the pavement, only adds to the charm.
Gouraud Street
+961 (0)1 585 586
lapizzariabeirut.com

⑪

Meat the Fish, Saifi Village
Crate food

Owner Karim Arakji started
out supplying premium
sustainable meat and fish
to hotels and restaurants
across Lebanon. From this
came the idea for Meat the
Fish: a gourmet butcher and
fishmonger where patrons can
also pull up a chair and enjoy
freshly cooked food.

 Wooden crates double as
display shelves for the day's
produce and outdoor furniture
for sun-worshippers. "I
wanted it to feel like a market
where you can touch and feel
things," says Arakji. This is a
place where quality counts for
everything; even the market
salad is phenomenal.
Moukhallassiya Street
+961 (0)5 441 205
meatthefish.com

⑫
La Petite Maison, Downtown
Je ne sais quoi

Beirut's Downtown district isn't wanting for high-end dining options but few manage to nail that combination of understated elegance and welcoming ambience as La Petite Maison does. Featuring soaring windows, with bowls of colourful produce lining the bar, the interior feels as light and modern as the food.

Its origins may be in Nice but the menu eschews heavier, creamy French fare in favour of Mediterranean dishes flavoured with herbs, lemon, tomatoes and olive oil. This is unfussy food that lets the quality of the ingredients shine. Reserve a space and don't miss the moreish Tomatinis. Perfect for a smart dinner.

*M1 building, Omar Daouk Street
+961 (0)1 999 380
lpmbeirut.com*

13
Al Hindi, Ein el Mraysseh
Indian feast

You'll find this restaurant
tucked away in the Warwick
Palm Beach Hotel on the
Corniche. The velvety chairs,
oriental rugs and deep red
decor may make Al Hindi feel
like a lavish, if slightly formal,
option. But what it lacks in
lively atmosphere it makes
up for in outstanding food:
samosas, vegetarian curries,
biryanis and raitas, all served
in rustic copper bowls.

Every dish is freshly
prepared so don't be afraid
to ask for adjustments to the
spiciness. Lunch is popular
but Al Hindi is best for dinner
with (hungry) friends.
Warwick Palm Beach Hotel,
Phoenicia Street
+961 (0)1 361 341
warwickhotels.com/palm-beach

14
Kissproof, Badaro
Best of the brunch

Despite sounding like a tacky
nightclub, this attractive little
café is easily one of the best
places to enjoy simple, good
food and a few drinks on the
up-and-coming Badaro Street.
Grab a table on the leafy
terrace and start the day with
a bowl of homemade granola,
or pair a crunchy salad with an
indulgent sourdough sandwich
for lunch.

Kissproof also has tasty
daily specials, including
charcuterie and desserts. Come
night-time it quickly fills up
with a young international
crowd who knock back craft
beers, cocktails and bowls of
delicious homemade pickles.
Badaro Street
+961 (0)1 382 992
kissproofbeirut.com

Coffee shops
Caffeinated culture

①
L'Atelier du Miel Workshop &
Garden Café, Mar Mikhael
Totally buzzing

This sun-soaked café branch
of the established Atelier du
Miel honey boutique is every
bit as sweet as it sounds.
Owner and architect Marc-
Antoine Bou Nassif wanted to
create a unique experience and
share his passion for honey.

The coffee can be sweetened
with seasonal unblended honey
from the mountains, coasts and
plains of Lebanon. In fact, all
of the menu features honey,
with a touch of thyme, orange
blossom or summer flowers
added to the simple but tasty
fare. You can also pick up
some gifts to take home at
the adjoining shop.
Armenia Street
+961 (0)1 565 975
atelierdumiel.com

②
Backburner, Saifi Village
Coffee with a bite

This small outpost in Saifi
Village boasts a New York-
style industrial interior, a
selection of the day's local
newspapers and fresh milk,
the latter a surprising scarcity
as many outposts opt for
UHT. The coffee menu ranges
from espressos and frappes to
French press and Turkish, with
all the good stuff imported
from London roastery Allpress.
There are coffee-free options
too, including a turmeric latte.

Owner and restaurateur
Karim Arakji (*see Maryool,
page 30*) also understands the
importance of good snacks,
stocking cardamom energy
balls and granola alongside
more indulgent bites such
as banana-tahini bread.
Ariss and Kanafani Street
+961 (0)1 989 343
thebackburner.com

Must-try
**Knafeh from Nemer al-Wadi
Sweets, Dar el Fatwa**
Melted cheese oozing out
from a golden semolina crust,
all soaking in sweet syrup.
This sticky treat usually comes
as dessert but at Nemer
al-Wadi it's also served as
a straight up sandwich.
+961 (0)1 741 931

Golden oldie
───
Historic chain Café Younes
has been serving the black
stuff since 1935. These days
its several Hamra branches are
frequented by students and
office workers attracted by
the laidback atmosphere and
extensive coffee menu.
cafeyounes.com

③
Kalei Coffee Co, Mar Mikhael
Micro-roastery

The first thing that will win
your affection at Beirut's
original micro-roastery is the
garden; the second is the smell
of coffee freshly roasting on
site. Co-owners Dalia Jaffal
and Andre Fadel source the
beans themselves from around
the world – from Honduras
to Ethiopia – with a bean-
to-cup business model that
ensures optimum quality
and traceability.

Whether you're after an
espresso, a v60 pour-over or
something a tad stronger (say,
a coffee-based cocktail spiked
with Italian Averna), Kalei
has you covered. To sweeten
the pot, throw in a great wine
and beer selection, creative
food options (arak-infused
marmalade on toast, anyone?)
and a traditional Lebanese
house setting.
Street 54, Impasse 18
+961 (0)3 780 342
kaleicoffee.com

Cone zone

**01 Hanna Mitri, Furn el
Hayek:** Open non-
stop since 1949 (even
during the 15-year civil
war), this no-frills shop
makes both traditional
mastic ice cream and
seasonal fruity sorbets
squashed into Lebanese
wafer cones.
+961 (0)1 322 723

02 Oslo, Mar Mikhael:
Notable for its
whitewashed sweet-
shop interior, Oslo uses
natural ingredients to
make more than 50
flavours. Its beautifully
packaged baked goods
are worth a try too.
osloicecream.com

**03 Orso Bianco, Furn el
Hayek:** Specialising
in gelato, this pretty little
place sells ice-cream
sandwiches and ice lollies
covered in chocolate,
as well as the traditional
scoops in a cone.
+961 (0)1 219 195

④
Street sellers, Ein el Mraysseh
True brew

If you want the real Arabic
coffee experience, leave
behind the hipster hubs of
Mar Mikhael, Hamra and
Saifi Village and head to the
Corniche. This is where people
from all walks of life fish, jog,
play music and share food,
and also where you'll find men
pushing wooden carts and
serving tiny cups of hot, fresh
Turkish coffee.

Made of finely ground
beans boiled on the spot, it's a
strong, bitter brew that's served
unfiltered, often with a touch of
cardamom. Just remember to
let the silt settle to the bottom
of your cup first.
Corniche

①
Souk el Tayeb, Downtown
Bumper harvest

Despite being in the glossy but
bland Beirut Souks open-air
mall, Souk el Tayeb is anything
but boring. Set up in 2004
by Kamal Mouzawak – the
man behind Tawlet restaurant
(*see page 27*) – it was the first
farmers' market in Lebanon,
promoting local organic food
back when Beirut was all about
hamburgers and sushi.

The small cluster of stalls
offers freshly made *saj* wraps,
mountain-grown vegetables,
fresh-pressed juice and
a smattering of artisanal
handicrafts. Everything is
sold by small producers from
across the country who are
only too happy to chat to you
about their recipes, ingredients
or local area. Come hungry on
Saturdays, from 09.00 to 14.00.
Trablos Street, Beirut Souks
+961 (0)1 442 664
soukeltayeb.com/souke-el-tayeb

②
House of Zejd, Furn el Hayek
Ancient roots

An olive-oil mecca, House
of Zejd is part of a family
business dating back to the
19th century. It sells three
types of extra-virgin oil, a
huge range of oils – infused
with everything from chilli
to white truffle – stuffed
olives, tapenade and even
some moreish olive jam, all
beautifully presented.

Zejd is Phoenician for "oil"
and the Fares family take their
culinary heritage seriously,
with the olives all grown and
harvested at their farm in
Akkar, north Lebanon. If
you want to learn more they
offer olive-picking trips from
November to December, as
well as tastings and tutorials
all year round.
Issa Building, Mar Mitr Street
+961 (0)1 338 003
zejd.net

③

Goodies, Verdun
Home comforts

A welcoming deli with a
popular adjoining café,
Goodies has everything in
abundance. Delicious cakes,
homemade Arabic sweets,
locally produced yoghurt
and cheese, and a menu
overflowing with options
to eat in or takeaway.

It's known for its home-style
Arabic dishes that few other
restaurants can match, such
as *mulukhiyeh*, a soup with
Jew's mallow (an edible leaf),
chicken stock and rice. The
Halwany family first opened
the shop in Downtown in 1880
and it has since been taken
over by successive generations,
moving to this location in 1979.
The owners are usually in the
shop, greeting clients by name.
Verdun Street
+961 (0)1 796 797
goodies.com.lb

The sweetest thing
—

A 140-year-old family business
specialising in Arabic *halawiyat*,
Amal Bohsali is a must for
travellers with a sweet tooth.
With three branches and super-
friendly staff, it's a cinch to
pick out your favourite Arabic
sweets, from crunchy baklava
to oozing *knafeh*.
abohsali.com.lb

Bars
Thirsty work

① Salon Beyrouth, Clemenceau
All that jazz

Inspired by 1920s jazz bars, Salon Beyrouth is peppered with art deco touches, from the ironwork on the doors to the geometric ceiling lamps. Set in the garden and first floor of an old Lebanese house, it captures a faded grandeur that appeals to a low-key crowd.

The bartenders specialise in whiskey cocktails but can make almost any tipple you like. There are weekly live performances – usually of jazz but also Brazilian and Latin music – and a DJ at weekends.
Mohammed Abdelbaki Street
+961 79 185 790
salonbeyrouth.com

Drink up
———

The fruits of Colonel Beer, Lebanon's most successful craft brewery, can be enjoyed throughout Beirut – just look out for bottles stamped with a pirate. If you're bored of lager, try the red ale. It's not quite the real thing but it's tasty nonetheless.
colonelbeer.com

On the tiles

01 **Beirut Groove Collective, citywide:** For vinyl-lovers and fans of deep funk, northern soul and African funk, this club night is a must. Events take place at different venues across town and are particularly popular among an alternative crowd.
+961 70 990 198

02 **B018, Karantina:** This legendary club only really gets going after 02.00, with DJs playing dance and techno until early morning. The crowning glory is when the sunken structure's roof lifts up to reveal the dawn sky.
+961 (0)1 580 018

03 **The Grand Factory, Karantina:** Perched in a former factory with panoramic views, this eccentric spot is made for dancing the night away among Beirut's glamorous party crowd. Saturday night's C U Nxt Sat events are very popular.
+961 3 703 371

04 **The Garten, Biel:** The summer version of nightlife stalwart Uberhaus, this alfresco venue boasts a four-sided island bar, food stalls and a honeycomb lighting structure under which party people rave to house and techno.
+961 76 363 662

05 **Decks on the Beach, Sporting Club, Ras Beirut** A Beirut summer classic. From May to September people gather at this outdoor cliff-edge club every weekend to enjoy the techno music in combination with a welcome sea breeze.
+961 70 856 866

③
Coop d'Etat, Gemmayzeh
Top of the world

So beloved by some Beirutis that it may as well be their living room, this large unpretentious rooftop bar is popular all day long. It's found several floors above Café Em Nazih (*see page 25*) and, while the stairs can be a killer in the middle of summer, the climb is undoubtedly worth the effort.

Coop d'Etat is a laidback place to catch the sunset over the port with a beer and a rather sinful plate of nachos, and one of the few rooftop bars in Beirut without a dress code. It's covered and heated in the winter and regularly hosts DJs at the weekend.
Saifi Urban Gardens, Pasteur Street
+961 71 134 173
saifigardens.com/en/rooftop

②
Dragonfly, Gemmayzeh
Old-school vibe

With its long wooden bar, faded orange-pink walls and curious window display of dried fruit, Dragonfly feels somewhere between a saloon and a Parisian bar. Either way it's a great place for a few drinks.

The bartenders are experts at every item on the extensive cocktail list, knocking out perfect rosemary whiskey sours and saké martinis all night long. Dragonfly attracts a professional but lively crowd who want to chat while they booze, usually with jazz playing softly in the background.
Gouraud Street
+961 (0)1 561 112

Work it!

④

Ferdinand, Hamra
Bourbon and burgers

A US-style bar stuffed with
tall wooden bar stools and
comfy sofas, Ferdinand can
be squeezy (and smoky) but
the energy is second to none.
The small space is a Hamra
institution thanks to the spirit
and vision of its owners.

Walid Merhi (*pictured,
bottom left*) mixes top-notch
cocktails of his own invention,
including the Imperial
Wolfhound with peated
Irish malt, bourbon and an
imperial stout reduction, while
Riad Aboulteif cooks mega-
indulgent "food from the
heart". The Ferdinand burger
with blueberry jam, cheese,
bacon and tarragon mayo is
a particular favourite. It also
stocks beer from the UK,
Germany and Belgium.
*Mahatma Gandhi Street
+961 (0)1 355 955*

⑤
Bardo, Clemenceau
Open to all

Named after the Tibetan Buddhist term for a state between death and rebirth, this café turns into a bar by night and hosts events that range from film screenings to poetry readings. It's also known for its eclectic music selection, chosen by some of Beirut's best DJs.

In addition to its warm atmosphere and rowdy evenings, since opening in 2006 Bardo has represented a safe space for the gay community in a country where homosexuality is still prohibited by law.
Mexico Street
+961 (0)1 340 060
bardobeirut.com

⑥
Centrale, Gemmayzeh
Architectural feat

Designed by well-known local architect Bernard Khoury, Centrale is found in a renovated 1920s home, with a French restaurant on the ground floor and a long tube-like structure perched above – this is where the bar is. Catch the lift, pull up a stool and order a cocktail or something from the French wine list.

It's a unique spot and worth visiting just for the moment when the roof windows slide back to reveal the city skyline. A high-end place with a dress code to match.
Takchi Building,
Mar Maroun Street
+961 (0)1 575 858
centrale-beirut.com

Sky's the limit

Skybar has had a few addresses but its current rooftop enclave overlooks the Mediterranean and can host up to 2,500 revellers. This nightlife mecca may require you to dress to the nines but its rota of big entertainment names is worth the effort.
skybarbeirut.com

Bars by neighbourhood

01 Mar Mikhael: Anise specialises in aniseed drinks or, to be specific, the Levantine liqueur of arak, and at night this dimly lit bolthole gets rather rowdy. The buzz from nearby Radio Beirut is unmissable, with live DJs and musicians playing late into the night.

02 Gemmayzeh: Tiny but lively dive-bar Torino Express (known as Torino's) is a must-visit whatever the time of night. Just around the corner, Demo is a more chilled option.

03 Ashrafieh: With a tasty wine menu and a bohemian vibe, Cantina Sociale makes a great stop for a few low-key drinks. Or try Bread Republic's cave-like Wine Room for a more romantic atmosphere.

04 Badaro: A visit to this leafy neighbourhood should begin with a beer on the terrace of local gem Roy's. Then try Attic Bar, a kitschy place crammed with random paraphernalia and intimate drinking spots.

05 Hamra: Oenologists should check out Cru Wine Bar's fantastic selection of Lebanese wines. Or grab a few beers at Li Beirut, a tiny but much-loved bar that also does great mezze.

06 Downtown: A favourite among well-heeled Beirutis, Iris Beirut's rooftop is an unrivalled place for a sundowner. Over in Biel, the famous open-air SkyBar is a spectacle well worth the price tag.

Retail
—— Shop 'til you drop

There's no shortage of opportunity to part with some cash while in Beirut. As well as a healthy quota from venerated design names such as Nada Debs, Bokja and Orient 499 (*see page 55*), the diverse retail offering is populated with small-scale fashion labels, many of which have been fostered through the creative-industry launchpad Starch Foundation (*see page 55*).

The city is also home to canny shop owners who have turned their attention to highlighting the many and varied artisan crafts in the region, rejigging tapestry-making, metalwork and tailoring for a more contemporary take on the traditional. And with a healthy representation of multi-brand men's and women's outposts, independent bookshops and vintage-furniture stop-offs, we guarantee your wallet will get a good workout.

①
Zawal, Mar Mikhael
Artisan acquisitions

On the eastern fringes of Mar Mikhael's retail and restaurant cluster is Zawal, which pulls together the work of some of the region's most talented but often overlooked artisans. The team in charge here is also behind the series of Beyt guesthouses, restaurant Makan (*see page 33*) and shop Plan Bey (*see page 55*), which has its original outpost next door.

This wide-reaching network is reflected in the shop's goods, which range from hand-stamped sheets by Zena Sabbagh to traditional mouth-blown recycled glass by Baal. "Zawal is home to works that we feel embody true Lebanese artisan culture," says co-founder Tony Sfeir.
Geara Building, Armenia Street
+961 (0)1 444 110

③
Liwan, Mar Mikhael
In-house creations

Designer Lina Audi opened the first Liwan boutique in Paris's Saint-Germain before branching out to Beirut. Here, surrounded by restaurants, bars and other retailers, her shop is well placed to show off its babouche slippers, loungewear and bed linen, as well as serving trays and bowls with modernist metalwork.

Liwan doubles as an interior-design showroom but Audi is perhaps best known for her clothing line – a modern take on traditional Middle Eastern fashion.
56 Madrid Street
+961 (0)1 444 141
liwanlifestyle.com

②
Orient 499, Clemenceau
Traditions updated

Frank Luca and Aida Kawas wanted to refresh the concept of craft and shift the products into a more modern sphere. Orient 499 is the result of their endeavours, a hybrid of the duo's penchant for the avant garde and their support for the preservation of Middle Eastern makers and cultural heritage.

"For such a small country, Lebanon is spoiled for talented designers," says Luca. It's an opinion he backs up with inventory from an impressive array of makers including jewellers, tailors and carpenters – all on display in this bright Clemenceau space.
499 Omar Daouk Street,
+961 (0)1 369 499
orient499.com

Small wonder
———
It may be petite but The Carton – the multi-brand shop from the makers of the eponymous magazine – has a big offering. Located in Kalei Coffee, it sells gear from Lebanon's new wave of makers. Fans of the title can also peruse copies on display.
artandthensome.com

④
Artisans du Liban et d'Orient, Ein el Mraysseh
Promoting regional craftsmanship

The late Nadia El-Khoury took over Artisans du Liban et d'Orient shortly after the death of its founder, May El-Khoury. She went on to become one of the first in the city to propose a contemporary interpretation of traditional oriental fare.

Beneath the whitewashed, vaulted ceilings of her tucked-away shop, coppersmiths, woodworkers, glass-blowers, soap-makers, weavers and embroiderers have all found a space to offer their goods new life. We recommend you plan a visit around sunset so you can peruse the wares before enjoying the seaside view from the pretty terrace, a Turkish coffee in hand.
Rafik Hariri Avenue
+961 (0)1 362 610

②
Ideo Parfumeurs, Gemmayzeh
Heaven scent

In 2006, French-Algerian Ludmila Bitar quit her job in L'Oréal's marketing head office and moved to Beirut with her Lebanese husband Antoine. With her marketing know-how and training from Japanese perfume house Takasago, the duo founded Ideo Parfumeurs in 2013 – a bold step in a city known for favouring big international cosmetic brands.

Just a year later Ideo opened its first shop to sell the bold scents and candles. "We're inspired by Beirut's contradictions, so we like to mix ingredients that don't normally go together," says Bitar. "It's a marriage of the orient and Europe."
Gouraud Street
ideoparfumeurs.com

①
Sarah's Bag, Sursock
Bags of conscience

The foundation of Sarah Beydoun's eccentric handbag label was laid during a prison visit she made in 2000 while researching for her sociology degree. Wanting to arm female prisoners with skills, an income and a project, Beydoun designed a series of bags and enlisted inmates to craft them.

The first exhibition of 12 bags sold instantly so Beydoun launched the label that has since grown to draw on a wealth of traditional design and employ more than 200 women. "We try to modernise crafts that we know exist in the region and push their boundaries to turn the bags into daily items," says Beydoun.
1F, Mhanna Building,
100 Lebanon Street
+961 (0)1 575 586
shop.sarahsbag.com

③
Rana Salam Studio,
Gemmayzeh
Pop star

While pursuing her MA at
the Royal College of Arts in
London, Rana Salam dedicated
her studies to Middle Eastern
popular culture. Aiming to
recapture lost pop visuals from
her home region, she began
unconsciously exporting her
culture to the West. "Through
the images people discovered
their own identity and fell in
love with the idea," she says.

After moving back to
Beirut in 2010, she remained
tied to the UK by founding
a cross-cultural studio that
specialises in branding and
design. Salam creates products
– from cushions printed
with Egyptian pop icons to
accessories carrying symbols
of contemporary street style
– that tell a story of Middle
Eastern pop culture, though
not without a wink of humour
and a nod to the kitsch.
Zoghbi Building, Lebanon Street
+961 (0)1 446 216
ranasalam.com

④
Iwan Maktabi, Furn el Hayek
Floor show

"Carpets in the Middle East
are like jewellery," says Chirine
Maktabi, the third-generation
executive manager of venerated
carpet seller Iwan Maktabi.
It's a sentiment reflected in
the showroom, with four floors
of rugs, many created by the
in-house design team. Crafted
in wool, silk, nettle, hemp and
felt, they span styles from
traditional Arabic patterns
to more modern motifs.

Running the business since
the 1920s, the Maktabis have
strong ties to the world's best
weavers and source their
carpets from Iran, Morocco
and more. The emphasis
remains on quality, with 90 per
cent of their stock handmade.
Quantum Tower,
Charles Malek Avenue
+961 (0)1 336 301
iwanmaktabi.com

Homeware
Inner pieces

① Ardeco, Furn el Hayek
Vintage to modern designs

This business was founded by architect Elie Amatoury in 1998, out of a passion for art deco, and now includes more than a century's worth of primarily European design history with pieces from the likes of Émile-Jacques Ruhlmann, Pierre Paulin and Ettore Sottsass. The glitzy new showroom has furniture and fixtures from the 1970s onwards, while the original Ardeco space across the street offers wares from art nouveau to postwar pop.

"We love creating a special atmosphere by mixing vintage pieces with contemporary design," says managing partner Georges Amatoury. "It makes for personalised interiors far from the 'catalogue look'."
79 Trabaud Street
+961 (0)1 338 785
ardeco.org

② Bokja, Saifi Village
Pieces with a wild side

The name of this Beirut-based brand – which comes from the Turkish word for the fabric that was historically used as a bride's dowry – was born when Huda Baroudi placed one of the antique textiles she had collected on top of a period chair that Maria Hibri was selling. That simple, fateful gesture led to a decades-long partnership marrying contemporary objects with ornate fabrics.

The founding duo (*both pictured, Baroudi on right*) also use their design work as a soapbox to speak out against social injustice.
332 Mukhallassiya Street
+961 (0)1 975 576
bokjadesign.com

③
Metal & Wood, Clemenceau
Small-batch furniture

The story of Metal & Wood, located in once-staid Clemenceau, is a familiar one. Founder Rached Sultan initially struggled to attract people to his shop when it opened in 2011 – whereas now the area is buzzing with retailers, galleries, guesthouses and cafés.

Sultan started off importing vintage furniture and then expanded the range to include homeware from both Japanese and Scandinavian labels. More recently, he has introduced his own line of furniture. "I want to produce small-batch stuff well, be an affordable brand but not skimp on materials," says Youssef.
105 America Street
+961 (0)1 367 480
metalandwoodstore.com

④
Nada Debs, Gemmayzeh
Cultural convergence

Nada Debs' product-design label predates her own life – or so the story goes. It is said that her great uncle went to China to seek a certain fabric, only to be redirected to Japan. There he settled, making the Debs one of the community's first Arab families.

Debs' designs reflect her efforts to fuse those two cultures. "It's about finding the balance between the two Easts," she says. The result is a unique union between extravagant Islamic aesthetics and Japanese simplicity.
Saad Building, Gouraud Street
+961 (0)1 568 111
nadadebs.com

⑤
Over the Counter, Monot
A focus on craftsmanship

In 2007, Rania Abillama Karam put the brakes on her career in truck-manufacturing to gear up for a personal venture. "I wanted to put my favourite things in life together under one roof," she says. Thus homeware shop Over the Counter was born as a space for dynamic design.

The team now sources its products from multiple design schools and countries, uniting emerging brands with special commissions. Pieces showcased in the sprawling three-level shop include vintage Danish furniture and Japanese crafts, as well as limited-edition and original designer pieces.
150 Abdel Wahab el Inglizi Street
+961 (0)1 322 786
over-thecounter.com

Three more furniture outposts

01 Karim Bekdache, Bourj Hammoud: Not only did Paris-trained architect Karim Bekdache design the layout for the Bourj Hammoud-based gallery and studio space D Beirut, he also displays his range of restored furniture inside it. Think pencil-legged sofas with mid-century echoes, as well as the occasional masterpiece by Jean Royère.
karimbekdache.com

02 Maria Halios, Mar Mikhael: Product and furniture designer Maria Halios is one of the artists who operates within Lebanon's new wave of contemporary homeware design. Visit Halios's Mar Mikhael showroom to see her collection, which both draws its influences from and marries together her Greek and Lebanese diasporas.
mariahalios.com

03 PSLab, Mar Mikhael: While it isn't a walk-in shop per se, the Nicolas Turk Street laboratory of this design brand has more than 80 people working inside to create lighting installations and products for site-specific projects – you'll see many examples in bars and shops across the city. The lighting label has also gone international, with studios in Stuttgart, London, Amsterdam, Antwerp, Dubai and Bologna.
pslab.net

⑥
Diwan Ammar, Basta
Oriental treasures

Piles of forgotten photos, calligraphy volumes, tarnished tea sets and ornate furniture lie cluttered in the souks and shopfronts of Basta, Beirut's top destination for antiques. Diwan Ammar is one of the neighbourhood's more refined retailers, with a history dating back to the 1940s.

Second-generation owner Youssef Ammar focuses mainly on Islamic pieces but more broadly on the oriental. The geographical spread on offer spans Lebanon, Turkey, Syria, Morocco and Iran while the archive has included such pieces as an Ottoman-style cabinet and a Baccarat crystal chandelier – not bad considering it was almost 200 years old.
Kharsa Street
+961 (0)1 658 483

❶
Ginette, Gemmayzeh
Furniture, fashion and food

This smart concept store combines fashion, homeware and art with healthy café fare. At the front of the space is a bistro-style restaurant, known for its labneh breakfast and farm-fresh lunch menu, while at the back is a retail area. The whole is seamlessly integrated by Lebanese firm Raëd Abillama Architects.

The shop carries furniture from the likes of Swiss firm USM and fashion by a rotating roster of both young Lebanese designers and more well-known labels. Up the concrete stairs, the second floor is home to Ginette's furniture and offices.
Gouraud Street
+961 (0)1 570 440
ginettebeirut.com

Now that's more like it...

③

Starch Foundation, Saifi Village
Emerging designers

Behind this ever-changing space is a non-profit organisation established by womenswear designer Rabih Kayrouz (*see page 59*) and Tala Hajjar in 2008. Their objective was to move the city's creative industries forward. "The burden of starting a business, whether here or elsewhere, is heavy – and emerging designers end up doing everything but focusing on the product, which is a shame," says Hajjar. "So we try and remove that burden."

The programme offers mentoring, press contacts and free use of the Saifi Village shopfront, meaning the roster of products is never the same, from fashion or lighting to artwork. The talent, however, is always fostered locally and has counted among its alumni Lara Khoury, Timi Hayek and Krikor Jabotian.
1051 Said Akel Street
+961 (0)1 566 079
starchfoundation.org

②

Plan Bey, Gemmayzeh
Looking good

Beirut-based publisher Plan Bey was founded in 2010 by graphic designer and artistic director Karma Tohmé and entrepreneur and editorial director Tony Sfeir. The duo has since opened three outposts across the city to sell their vibrant publications, which range from books to prints.

"Everything displayed in the shops, with very few exceptions, is created by us," says Tohmé. She and Sfeir draw inspiration from vintage film posters, calligraphy, photographs and more.
Gouraud Street
+961 (0)1 444 110
plan-bey.com

Mixed fashion
His and hers

② IF Boutique, Port District
Legendary leather

Sadly there's not enough space here to detail the life and escapades of leather designer and IF owner Johnny Farah (*pictured*). Rubbing shoulders with Arne Jacobsen and Fritz Hansen, and having lunch with Andy Warhol, is just a taster.

Farah started out helping a leather worker for pocket money while studying mechanical engineering in Denmark in the 1960s – today, he's still designing handsome and practical bags and shoes. Helped by his sisters, Farah is courageous in his choices, buying from designers early and taking a chance with the clothing he stocks.
Fayad Building, Darvich Haddad Street
+961 (0)1 570 244
ifsohonewyork.com

① LE66, Downtown
French evolution

The original Parisian home of LE66, and the source of its name, is 66 Avenue des Champs-Elysées. The French boutique hub launched its Lebanese outpost in the heart of Beirut's downtown shopping district in 2015. Architect Isabelle Stanislas collaborated with artist Patricia Marshall on the interiors and sought inspiration from Beirut's many faces, creating a space where smart copper shelves and marble tables contrast with raw concrete walls.

Shoppers can expect four floors of youthful threads, shoes and accessories for men and women, from brands such as Yeezy, Aspesi, Giorgio Brato and Être Cécile. It's this selection that has positioned LE66 Beirut at the heart of what the group's joint CEO Cherif Tabet has called "affordable luxury".
151 Foch Street
+961 (0)1 985 470
le66.fr

③
Lara Khoury, Gemmayzeh
Fashion statements

After kickstarting her career in 2010 with the help of Rabih Kayrouz (*see page 59*) and Tala Hajjar's fashion launchpad Starch Foundation (*see page 55*), Lara Khoury (*pictured*) has garnered a reputation as one of the city's most promising (and outspoken) designers. While style in the Middle East can veer towards the flamboyant, Khoury's range of men's and womenswear has found a tasteful balance, offsetting flamboyant fabrics with pared-back cuts or creating extravagant garments in quieter tones.

"Clients here are extravagant, they aren't afraid of wearing voluminous and statement pieces," says Khoury. Phone ahead to ensure a viewing of Khoury's contemporary collections in her Gemmayzeh studio.
406 Gouraud Street
+961 (0)1 443 426
larakhoury.com

④
6:05, Furn el Hayek
Party dress

This lively retail stop-off is well known not only for finding and fostering homegrown streetwear labels but also for hosting after-work parties at – you guessed it – 18.05. Label launches, collaboration events and more vague merriment in the name of celebrating design are reason enough for the DJ booth and pop-up bar to appear kerbside.

The two-storey shop stocks all of the regular international streetwear contenders but it's the young Lebanese brands that pull the crowds. The buyers at 6:05 play to this strength, managing to secure exclusive lines for both men and women.
Zen Building, Charles Malek Avenue
+961 (0)1 335 450
605.com.lb

La belle vie
―
The team at Furn el Hayek's The Good Life is on the ball when it comes to trainers; think kicks from limited production runs, interesting collaborations and hard-to-find brands. A little off the beaten track, it's for the real fanatics.
thegoodlifespace.com

Aïshti, Downtown

Tony Salamé first became a prominent name in Lebanon in 1989, when his first Aïshti department store entered the luxury retail market; later he would attract attention for his (arguably) ostentatious private gallery the Aïshti Foundation (*see page 88*). Now his multi-brand department store has five locations nationwide and more than 20 franchises in destinations such as Dubai, Kuwait and Amman.

On home soil, the most central Aïshti location is in the Solidere-renovated Beirut Souks in Downtown. Here you'll find five floors dedicated to high-end men's, women's and some kidswear from the likes of Gucci, Prada and Dries Van Noten. There's also a restaurant, spa and hair salon.
aishti.com

Menswear
Look sharp

②
Trunk, Saifi Village
Innovative styles

This multi-brand shop was founded by Marilyn Bouchakjian in 2013 before being snapped up by Beirut's menswear protagonists Pia and Nadim Chammas in 2016. The assembly of labels is contemporary and on point with what's emerging at the latest major fashion weeks.

"Our customers are demanding," says Nadim. "They come to Trunk to find the most modern and innovative labels, with a clean style and high-quality manufacturing." Expect threads from the likes of Officine Générale and Ron Dorff, plus a hoard of shoes, eyewear, bags and fragrances.
Mkhallsiyeh Street
+961 (0)1 973 347
trunkconceptstore.com

①
The Slowear Store, Downtown
Timeless pieces

Operating under Venice-based parent brand Slowear, the Beirut outpost was brought to town by Pia and Nadim Chammas. Opening in 2012, it helped plug a gap in the market. "There were few local multi-brand shops dedicated to men; most of the attention was focused on the women's market," says Nadim.

Unlike the Chammas' other shop Trunk (*see right*), which favours young brands that follow the trends, Slowear carries more established labels such as Incotex, Montedoro and Zanone. "Each of these does one thing – trousers, shirts, jackets and knitwear – and one thing only," says Nadim. "And they do it very well."
Patriarch Howayek
+961 (0)1 999 230
slowear.com

Womenswear
Dress to impress

①
Plum, Downtown
International and edgy

Since opening Plum in 2004, co-owners Raya Dernaika and Mira Mikati have made it their mission to find "the beautiful and non-clichéd". Via their bricks-and-mortar shop, the pair have succeeded not only in making the brand an expression of who they are – forward-thinking – but also a power player in Lebanese womenswear retail.

The space encompasses an impeccably selected international wardrobe of high-end labels such as Monse, Alaïa, Balmain, Christopher Kane and Rosie Assoulin, as well as contemporary creations by the likes of Jacquemus, JW Anderson and Sacai. The sleek fit-out is care of homegrown architect Raëd Abillama.
Berytus Building, Fakhry Bey Street
+961 (0)1 976 565
plumconcept.com

Piaff, Clemenceau
Pushing the boundaries

In the early 1980s, Najla and Sosi Maatouk opened Piaff in Beirut with the objective of satisfying women who "wanted to express themselves differently and not follow trends systematically," says son and current owner Nabil Al Houssami. Since then, the shop has introduced pioneering European designers into the Lebanese market, including Simone Rocha.

Even today, with an inventive space, innovative displays and audacious selection, Piaff maintains an edge that places it on the fringes of the mainstream market.
Clemenceau Street
+961 (0)1 362 368

③
Maison Rabih Kayrouz, Port District
High-fashion hero

Rabih Kayrouz has played a key role in the development of Lebanon's haute couture scene. Since founding his label in 1997, he has crafted season after season of minimal yet sculptural dresses. He's also a co-founder of fashion launchpad Starch Foundation (*see page 55*) and was a member of the Chambre Syndicale de la Haute Couture in Paris.

In 2009 the brand moved its offices to Paris's Saint Germain, where it also has an atelier and showroom. Kayrouz continues to live between Beirut and Paris and his ethereal pieces are equally at home in both cities.
Fayad Building, Darwish Haddad Street
+961 (0)1 444 221
maisonrabihkayrouz.com

Bookshops
Bound to impress

Three more Beirut-based womenswear designers

01 Timi Hayek, Monot: Sitting alongside breezy cafés and restaurants on Monot Street, Timi Hayek's bright and tidy space is where she sells her relaxed ready-to-wear collections and tailored made-to-order garments. Hayek is another to have started her business with help from the Starch Foundation (*see page 55*). *timihayek.com*

02 Vanina, Gemmayzeh: Playful womenswear label Vanina can be found in a whitewashed shop on Gouraud Street. Tatiana Fayad and Joanne Hayek launched the brand with a single jewellery line in 2007 but the offering has grown to include on-trend cuts and bold fabrics. The entire range is made in Lebanon. *vanina.me*

03 Krikor Jabotian, Furn el Hayek: By the tender age of 23, Krikor Jabotian had graduated from university, worked in Elie Saab's creative department, designed his first collection with the guidance of the Starch Foundation (seeing a pattern yet?) and launched his eponymous atelier. Jabotian then brought his family on board to expand the business, a move which has seen his range of high-end evening gowns and bridalwear travel all the way to Hollywood. *krikorjabotian.com*

Bookshops
Bound to impress

1 Papercup, Mar Mikhael
Well-stocked selection

Rania Naufal's bookshop-cum-café was years in the making. She let the concept bubble away while studying publishing at NYU and working at the partly family-owned magazine and book wholesaler Levant Distributors. Then, in June 2009, she struck out on her own and opened her bolthole bookshop in a Mar Mikhael sidestreet.

The cosy space, designed by FaR Architects and Karim Chaya, features a magazine stack and catalogue of design, architecture, art, cinema, fashion, photography, advertising and kids' books that would give any leading major city bookshop a run for its money.
*Agopian Building, Pharaon Street
+961 (0)1 443 083
papercupstore.com*

②
Aaliya's Books, Gemmayzeh
Temple of literature

Expats and pals Niamh
Fleming-Farrell and William
Dobson were frustrated by
the predictable selection of
English-language books in
the city's chain retailers. "One
evening, after drinking a fair
amount of whiskey, we realised
that this was something we
both felt," says Dobson. "So,
we decided then and there to
open a bookshop."

The idea expanded from
a bookshop inside a café to
the duo buying the café and
tailoring the entire space to
celebrate literature. As for
the books, the well-read staff
have stocked their favourites,
including a mixture of
contemporary, classics, poetry
and a healthy selection of
regional novelists.
The Alleyway, Gouraud Street
+961 (0)1 566 375

Always room for
one more!

③
Dar Bistro & Books,
Clemenceau
A piece of quiet

This serene hideaway is a few
blocks from the hectic drag of
Hamra Street. The lounge-like
bookshop, complete with leafy
patio café, is an anomaly in
the city and therefore favoured
by local bookworms.

As well as international
fiction, magazines (including
MONOCLE), coffee-table
tomes and special-interest
publications, there's a section
dedicated to Lebanese history.
Dar also hosts regular book
launches, readings and
community events.
Alley 83 off Roma Street
+961 (0)1 373 348
darbistroandbooks.com

④
The Little Bookshop, Hamra
Small space, big appeal

Given its diminutive
proportions, The Little
Bookshop offers a mighty
selection for English literature
in the heart of Hamra. Owner
and sole employee Adib Rahhal
had dreamed of opening a
bookshop since his college days
and handpicks the collection of
contemporary fiction, classics,
poetry and non-fiction.

Also among the stacks of
titles piled floor to ceiling are
smaller selections on the arts,
cinema and music. Best call
ahead because Rahhal keeps
loose opening hours.
Makdisi Building,
Jeanne d'Arc Street
+961 (0)1 740 270

Things we'd buy
—— Talking shop

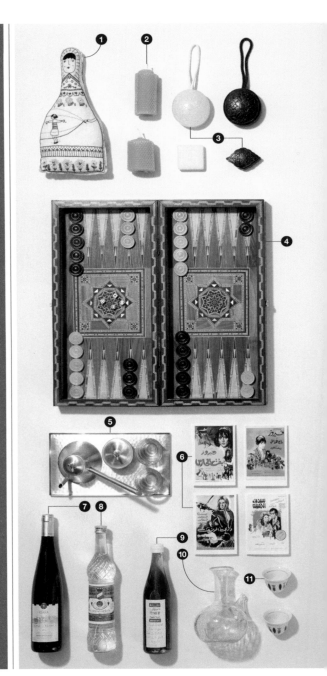

There's a bagful of opportunities to spend big while in Beirut. The abounding creative scene mixed with that unabashed Lebanese entrepreneurial spirit means there's always an interesting collaboration or social project producing tempting goods, whether it be a calligraphy book published by Plan Bey or embroidered dolls inspired by the stories of refugees.

Then there's a cohort of venerated brands – including Liwan, Nada Debs and Senteurs d'Orient – that weave Lebanese craftwork and aesthetics into contemporary clothing, homeware and soaps. And let's not forget a few tasty treats for the larder, so the flavours of Lebanon can linger long after you leave.

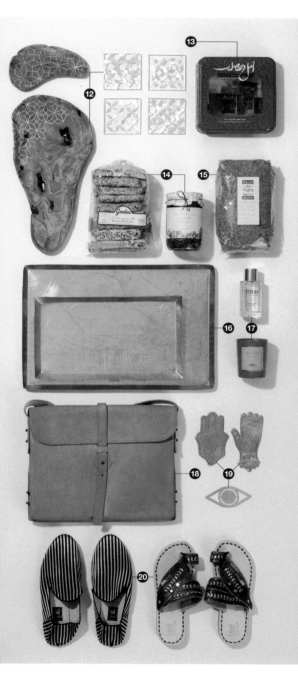

01 Embroidered doll by
The Ana Collection
theanacollection.org
02 Natural beeswax candles
from Zawal
+961 (0)1 444 110
03 Senteurs d'Orient
soaps from Artisan du
Liban et d'Orient
+961 (0)1 875 416
04 Backgammon board
from Artisanat Chehab
+961 3 561 451
05 Yellow copper coffee set
by Orient 499
orient499.com
06 Lebanese film postcards
from Plan Bey
plan-bey.com
07 Château Ksara Blanc de
Blancs from Score Market
+961 (0)1 344 411
08 Arak Touma from Score
Market *+961 (0)1 344 411*
09 Rose water from Tawlet
soukeltayeb.com/tawlet
10 Baal carafe from Zawal
+961 (0)1 444 110
11 Coffee cups from Takkoush
Verdun Street
12 Wooden boards and mother-
of-pearl coasters by Nada Debs
nadadebs.com
13 Baklava from Amal Bohsali
abohsali.com.lb
14 Crackers and fig jam
from Goodies
goodies.com.lb
15 Zaatar herb mix from Tawlet
soukeltayeb.com/tawlet
16 Chiselled brass trays
by Liwan
liwanlifestyle.com
17 Fragrances and candles
by Ideo Parfumeurs
ideoparfumeurs.com
18 Johnny Farah satchel from
IF Boutique
+961 (0)1 570 244
19 Hamsa and evil eye
talismans by Orient 499
orient499.com
20 Men's slippers and
women's sandals by Liwan
liwanlifestyle.com

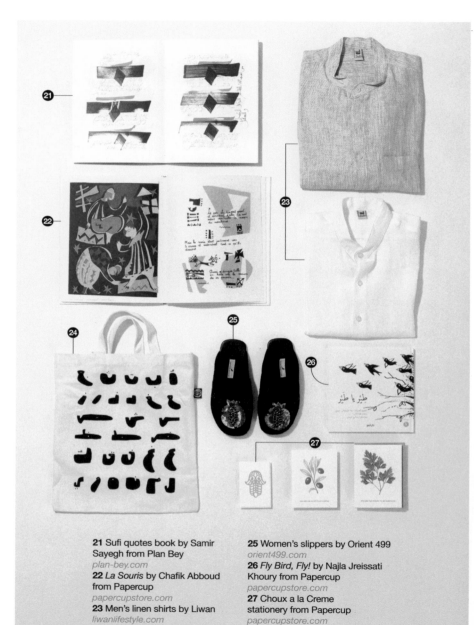

21 Sufi quotes book by Samir
Sayegh from Plan Bey
plan-bey.com
22 *La Souris* by Chafik Abboud
from Papercup
papercupstore.com
23 Men's linen shirts by Liwan
liwanlifestyle.com
24 Luanaric Arabic script tote
from Tawlet
soukeltayeb.com/tawlet

25 Women's slippers by Orient 499
orient499.com
26 *Fly Bird, Fly!* by Najla Jreissati
Khoury from Papercup
papercupstore.com
27 Choux a la Creme
stationery from Papercup
papercupstore.com

10 essays
—— Blueprints
of Beirut

1
At war with itself
Beirut's ups and downs
Carole Corm,
writer

2
Maiden voyage
Love at first sight
Sally Moussawi,
writer

3
Once more with feeling
Lebanese pop music
Tomos Lewis,
Monocle

4
Where the streets
have no names
Navigating Beirut
Bahi Ghubril,
entrepreneur

5
Mixing it up
Lebanese cuisine
Kamal Mouzawak,
writer and restaurateur

6
History in the making
Monumental decisions
Nasri Atallah,
writer

7
The kindness of strangers
Lebanese hospitality
Venetia Rainey,
Monocle

8
Unwritten rule
The politics at play
Christopher Lord,
writer

9
Seeking serenity
Quiet spaces in the city
Tala Hajjar,
entrepreneur

10
Raising the bar
Liquid Lebanon
Alex Rowell,
writer

*Mmm, nothing
gets my creative
juices flowing
like a cup of
Turkish coffee*

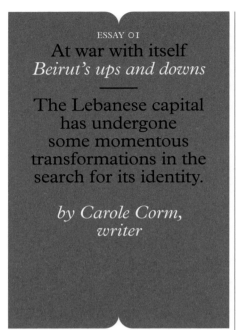

ESSAY 01
At war with itself
Beirut's ups and downs

The Lebanese capital has undergone some momentous transformations in the search for its identity.

by Carole Corm,
writer

Veering from vibrant capital city to warzone and back, Beirut has a schizophrenic reputation. Locals may deride such clichés yet the city's history comprises an undeniable cycle of highs and lows.

Prehistoric traces of the city go back some 40,000 years, although things really took off when the Phoenicians built city-states along the Lebanese coast about 4,000 years ago. This mighty civilisation founded cities such as Tyre, Byblos and Sidon but also left its mark on Beirut, building an imposing sea wall and port.

In 1271BC the Beirutis called on Egypt's Ramses II for help against the invading Hittites. While great seafarers, traders and even the inventors of the modern alphabet, the Phoenicians were not known for their prowess on the battlefield. The pharaoh obliged and his passage is inscribed on the banks of the Dog River, about 10km north of Beirut.

When the Romans arrived in 64BC they immediately took a shine to the city, naming it after the emperor's daughter.

Colonia Julia Augusta Felix Berytus became part university town – with one of the best law schools in the empire – and part retirement destination for decorated generals. This golden era came to an end in 551 when a terrible earthquake followed by a tsunami razed the city to the ground.

Beirut licked its wounds, slowly recovering under the Byzantines, then in the 7th century a succession of empires brought Islam to the Lebanese coast. Its arrival prompted religious minorities (first the Shia then the Druze) to join the Christian Maronites in nearby Mount Lebanon. In 1110 the fanaticised Crusaders descended on Beirut, killing its inhabitants after they resisted courageously. John of Ibelin later rebuilt the city and encouraged trade with Venice and Genoa but it was under Saladin and his Mamluk forces that the Franks were ultimately driven out, although trade with the West continued.

When the Ottoman Turks took over in 1515 they were content to collect their taxes, leaving local emirs to rule (unless they became too big for their boots). Things changed, however, when the ideas of the Enlightenment reached the Ottoman empire and Beirut became a testing ground for Ottoman modernisation.

"Beach clubs and modern hotels opened their doors on the promenade while Edith Piaf performed in shiny new music halls"

Roads, schools and hospitals were built while missionaries, mostly French and American, opened prestigious universities.

By the end of the 19th century a "republic of merchants" had emerged and, like Smyrna and Alexandria, Beirut became the quintessential Levantine city, open to the world for business and play. This boom was cut short by the First World War, as famine and conscription decimated the population and Lebanese nationalists were hunted down. When the war ended, the UK and France redrew the map of the Middle East. Mount Lebanon with its Christian and Francophile population lobbied for a new state: Le Grand Liban, with Beirut as its capital.

The city took on the airs of the French Riviera. Beach clubs and modern hotels opened their doors on the promenade, while Edith Piaf performed in shiny new music halls. Armenians who had suffered ethnic cleansing under the Turks created an industrious new neighbourhood, confirming Lebanon as a haven for minorities.

Despite the epicurean culture they brought with them, the French were nonetheless a colonial power and in 1943 Lebanon gained its independence from them. Now "The Paris of the Middle East" would see to its own affairs, surfing on the nascent oil boom and becoming a major banking centre.

Yet those Lebanese who favoured the Pan-Arab Egyptian leader Nasser saw the country as too western and liberal and, in 1958, a miniature civil war erupted. By the next decade the increasing power of Palestinian fedayeen in Lebanon's refugee camps upset the balance of power between Muslims and Christians and, in 1975, war erupted again, with international powers waltzing in and out of the hostilities. Beirut divided along religious lines with a Christian East and a Muslim West.

When the war ended in 1990, Beirut was an eerie collection of bombed-out buildings. Reconstruction was on the agenda, spearheaded by Rafik Hariri, a maverick businessman turned prime minister. Following a controversial plan, the city centre was rebuilt with the help of a roster of international architects.

Today, Downtown is a gleaming showcase for the country. Critics may decry the upscale commercial atmosphere but the result is nonetheless impressive. Hariri, meanwhile, was assassinated in 2005 in a massive explosion that shook the city and redrew the political landscape. His murder led to protests demanding the exit of Syria, Lebanon's de facto ruler since the end of the 1975 to 1990 civil war.

In 2006, Hezbollah and Israel fought a short but destructive war that saw South Lebanon and Beirut's southern suburbs (Dahieh) destroyed, although they were to be rebuilt in record time. Then simmering differences between Hezbollah's supporters and the political faction led by Hariri's son led to a prolonged sit-in by the former in the city centre. In 2008 the opposing camps took to the streets and a return to civil war was only narrowly avoided.

Somehow none of these events halted development. On its outskirts Beirut has grown exponentially but mostly chaotically, with a lack of agreement on what blueprint to follow, if any. Should Beirut be like Dubai? Tehran? Las Vegas? Meanwhile more than a million Syrian refugees fleeing the nearby war have put pressure on the infrastructure of the country and its capital. Feuding politicians and corruption have not helped matters, failing to provide citizens with basic services.

For all its reversals of fortune, however, Beirut maintains a charm all of its own, one that will likely never fade. It's an unruly mix of old and new, East and West, that defies a turbulent history. — (M)

Beirut's top tunes

01 'Alo Beirut', Saba
Searching for love across town in an impossibly retro song.
02 'Li Beirut', Fairuz
An ode to the war-torn city by Lebanon's most famous singer.
03 'Beirut', Yasmine Hamdan
The indie chanteuse laments the changing face of her hometown.

ABOUT THE WRITER: Carole Corm is a writer and former MONOCLE correspondent, and author of *Beirut – A Guide to the City*.

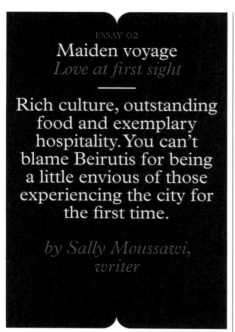

ESSAY 02

Maiden voyage
Love at first sight

———

Rich culture, outstanding food and exemplary hospitality. You can't blame Beirutis for being a little envious of those experiencing the city for the first time.

by Sally Moussawi, writer

Beirut is salty, humid air, streets jammed with traffic and footpaths filled with revellers spilling out of lively bars. It's public spaces run by gangs of valets and shopkeepers milling in doorways, ready to greet you with a warm smile. For the uninitiated it's a sensory barrage that can be frenetic and relentless – but that same eclectic onslaught is what seduces maiden voyagers. If this is your first trip to Beirut, I envy you.

It's true what they say: contradictions reign supreme here. But not the oversimplified dichotomies, such as mosques and churches standing side by side or a society that's at once liberal and regressive. In Beirut the contradictions are in the details.

Unchecked urbanisation and years of chaotic postwar construction grind against the vast Mediterranean to the west and the bucolic Mount Lebanon skyline to the east; the smell of the city's battle with rubbish is soothed by the scent of jasmine; and the roar of private electricity generators is outperformed by birdsong. A frenzied, contradictory energy pulsates through Beirut. In this small historic city, everything is confronted with itself in a claustrophobic but thrilling way, each detail an antidote for its opposite. The result is unique, comical and – bizarrely – calming.

For culture-lovers, Beirut is a city of unimaginable talent that boasts a thriving art and creative scene. Its gifted denizens include new-generation fashion designers Sara Melki and Krikor Jabotian, and entrepreneurial ventures Karma Tohmé and Bey Group. Art foundations Ashkal Alwan and the Beirut Art Center brush shoulders with modern-art museums Dar El-Nimer and Saleh Barakat. It's a roll-call of talent that fans the fabulous flames of cultural vibrancy, cementing Beirut's position as the creative capital of the Middle East and attracting increasing international visibility.

Food fans, I reserve my strongest envy for you. The real sense of Lebanese emotion is captured in its cuisine, from the simple and raw ingredients such as crunchy *me'teh* (muskmelon, not cucumber) and juicy kibbeh (provenance is key) to the complicated and elaborate fervour of dishes served at cool concept restaurants such as Maryool (*see page 30*) and Kharouf. Then there are more sobering plates such as the *fetteh* (thick yoghurt with soft chickpeas) from Abou Hassan (*see page 29*) in Bourj Hammoud – perfect at dawn as you roll out of late-night dance temple AHM.

In Beirut the smell of food triggers emotions and floods you with memories: the aroma of freshly baked *manoushe* on an alleyway corner and the scent of fried Sultan Ibrahim fish in upscale restaurants such as Babel sur Mer or at cosy old-timers such as the canteen in Sporting Club (*see page 122*). Sometimes even sound is enough to whet the appetite – the chants of the *kaak* bicycle man on the Corniche, promising cream cheese on a fresh sesame bread roll, or the bubbling of oil frying falafel balls at Falafel Sahyoun.

> "*A frenzied, contradictory energy pulsates through Beirut. In this small historic city, everything is confronted with itself in a claustrophobic but thrilling way*"

All this may sound too good to be true and, in a way, it is. Beirut isn't without its problems. There's regional and international political instability, systemic corruption, surreal social inequality and deteriorating infrastructure (more and more homes are supplied with salty water due to poor access to fresh alternatives). The gridlocked traffic, meanwhile, drives even the most pious to *kaafer* (a state of anger, disbelief and the renouncing of God on a daily basis).

But while Beirut doesn't operate the way most well-oiled cities do, its unguarded and foolhardy vibe make it common for visitors to comment that the city feels "alive". It *is* alive – and those who live here feel it too. There's something special at work in this city, like a cocktail of good and bad, of a defiant passion for life and a drive for self-destruction, blended with a sense of the fleetingness of it all.

So, *ahlan wa sahlan*. This is a terribly exciting city – and we are terribly excited to welcome you to it. — (M)

Smells like home
—
01 **Blossoming jasmine**
Most fragrant on warm summer evenings.
02 **'Saboun baladeh'**
Lebanese soap; think clean sheets and warm baths.
03 **'Manoushe'**
Freshly baked and topped with zaatar.

ABOUT THE WRITER: MONOCLE-raised Sally Moussawi is a writer by fancy and a project manager by profession. She was born in Beirut and often wonders why she continues to trade in the sunny climes of Lebanon for the drizzly UK.

ESSAY 03

Once more with feeling
Lebanese pop music

———

It may have an assured market abroad thanks to the country's diaspora but it's at home that Lebanese pop truly soars, acting as an emotional outlet and counterpoint to the city's turmoil.

by Tomos Lewis,
Monocle

It was a balmy evening in late spring of 2008 and I was sitting in a neighbour's apartment just outside Beirut. The rickety air-conditioning was battling the warm air that slipped in through the open balcony window, which hung over the rowdy bustle of the coastal highway below.

We were watching TV after work, drinking cold Almaza. This had become a little ritual during the nine months or so since I'd moved to Lebanon to work as an editor at a publishing house. A commercial break interrupted our programme but instead of the jingly ads for car dealerships or supermarkets, a short film began to play.

It was slightly melancholic despite the rose-tinted snapshots of Beirut and Lebanon it offered. There was sweeping footage of Pigeon's Rock and the cedar woodlands stretching up into the ridges to the city's west, as well as shots of the coastline, the mountains, wineries and children playing in a village square.

The soundtrack to these nostalgic postcards of Lebanon and its capital was a song I'd heard before: "Ya Beirut" by Majida El Roumi, pop royalty in Lebanon for some 40 years. Her song praised the beauty of the city while mourning the darker chapters in its history. If Beirut could have an anthem, my friend said, then this would probably be it. "Oh, Beirut! Oh Beirut!" Majida pined, as the montage of better days in Lebanon whipped by on the screen. "You are the grandmother of the world… [But] we didn't understand you. We didn't spare you. We gave you a knife instead of a flower. Oh, Beirut!"

Films such as this have often been played on national television during troubled moments in Lebanon's recent history, counterpoints to national turmoil. That evening it provided respite from news coverage of the worst internal sectarian violence in Lebanon for more than a decade. The skyline of the city, seen from my friend's balcony, was fringed with wisps of smoke. In the streets, gunfights were being waged between fighters loyal to Hezbollah and the political party of then prime minister Saad al-Hariri. If this current bout of fighting held a grim familiarity for many in Lebanon, so too did the presence of Majida El Roumi and other popstars, on radio and television.

"Blasting from cars, from radios, in cafés – for different groups across the country, music is a way of identifying with something"

"At the time these songs were really emotional," says music historian Ayman Mhanna, recalling the broadcast of heartfelt songs during the years of Lebanon's 1975 to 1990 civil war. "Many people, including my family, lived outside Beirut and didn't have access to the city because of the war, because of the situation on the ground, because of the militias that controlled different territories within such a tiny place. So the idea of singing to Beirut – the city that was destroyed, the city that had been so envied – definitely had an impact on people."

El Roumi in particular is a flagbearer for these types of songs: her career began and flourished during the course of the 15-year civil war. In the months leading up to the crisis of 2008 I'd developed a quiet obsession with the star. I'd been urged by my new colleagues to listen to Lebanese pop songs – and to listen to them religiously – as an easy introduction to learning Lebanese Arabic.

My list of unlikely tutors included Fairuz, the most treasured of Lebanon's songstresses, whose prolific catalogue of songs covered subjects from love and the Lebanese landscape to narratives from Lebanon's recent past. She was joined by Nancy Ajram, cloyingly cheerful and, I was told, the classiest in Lebanon's pantheon of pop princesses at the time. Also making an appearance was Elissa, with her catchy, upbeat tales of heartbreak and love lost, and the raunchiest of them all, Haifa Wehbe, whose outfits were as scant as the musical merits of her oeuvre. But for me, El Roumi's soaring soprano, so unusual among the low-range singing in Arabic music, triumphed above all.

"She is lucky and unlucky at the same time," says Mhanna. "Lucky because she chose songs that had a very strong romantic and patriotic connotation; she was someone people could escape to. But unlucky, in a way, because her career falls between the generations; her top days of fame were during the war so even if she sings beautiful songs today, she's still associated with that period." The crisis of 2008 ended with the signing of the Doha Accord, which allowed the then army general Michel Suleiman to assume the presidency. The streets reopened and the nostalgic, patriotic music videos by El Roumi and her counterparts quietly slipped off the airwaves.

Pop music – and music more broadly in Lebanon – has long reflected life in the country. From the melodies of the seafarers inspired by the coastline to the *zajal* form of poetic singing prevalent in the mountains, "music is always somewhere in Lebanon",

says musician and musicology professor Youmna Saba. "Songs blasting from cars, from radios, in cafés – for different groups across the country it's a way of identifying with something."

Pop in Lebanon is also a major export; the estimated 14 million people who form the Lebanese diaspora ensure that its popstars have footholds in music markets from Brazil to Belgium, Canada to the Caribbean. At home too it's a significant player in the cultural economy; most of the region's major music shows and talent contests are filmed here, including the fabled *Studio El Fan*, which launched in 1972 and has given Majida and many of Lebanon's most successful music acts their first shots at fame.

"Because Lebanon has long enjoyed levels of social freedom that were much higher than anywhere else in the region, it allowed for much more audacity in how singers looked and what they sang about," says Mhanna. "This combination of both artistic quality and the audacity in how people look has made Lebanon a powerhouse in the region for pop music." — (M)

Pop princesses

01 Fairuz
The greatest of them all, born in 1935.

02 Nancy Ajram
The classiest fixture in Lebanon's pop pantheon.

03 Haifa Wehbe
Famed for her erotic songs.

ABOUT THE WRITER: Tomos Lewis is MONOCLE's bureau chief in Toronto. He worked for Lebanese publishing house Librairie du Liban from 2007 to 2008 and the bedrock for much of his Lebanese Arabic is still Majida El Roumi lyrics.

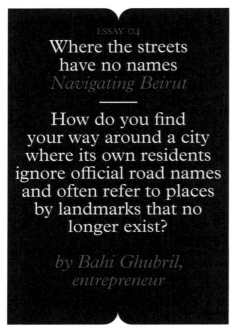

ESSAY 04

Where the streets have no names
Navigating Beirut

How do you find your way around a city where its own residents ignore official road names and often refer to places by landmarks that no longer exist?

by Bahi Ghubril, entrepreneur

"Meet me by the streetside café next to the French bistro in the heritage house with the red shutters at the end of the street where the big olive tree stands. There's a Chateau Wardy advert on the billboard on the main road – you'll see it from the new ABC mall towards the Saudi Embassy's old location."

This chaotic means of direction is normal in Beirut. We navigate by some strange hierarchical system, from the big landmarks down to smaller points of reference that change over time (and so indicate the latest fashionable hangouts or architectural must-sees).

Within this informal hierarchy, landmarks are ranked with government department buildings, foreign embassies and religious sites on top, followed by hospitals and universities, which guide you towards a general neighbourhood. Next come commercial centres and schools, then banks, petrol stations and pharmacies for more exact navigation, down to billboards, building sites and even valets, which can almost pinpoint a building or house. It's our address system, used for everything from business meetings to food deliveries, even by the emergency services.

Up until the 1940s, Beirut's streets were simply known for a prominent local family or landmark. But after independence a committee was created to assign them formal names. Some, such as Bustros Street and Central Bank Street, kept the names of the families who had lived there or the main landmarks they were known for. Others took on the names of newer political heroes, cultural figures (Mozart Street) or countries (Uruguay Street).

The problem remains, however, that these names are not displayed at street level – and when they are they're often rendered invisible by clutter and advertising. In some cases gangs of residents simply ignore a street's new designation. Rapid changes in the urban landscape, caused by the 1975 to 1990 civil war's shifts in demographics and dizzying cycles of destruction and rebuilding, have led to directions that rely on the collective memory of residents. One long road in the Hamra district, for example, is officially Baalbek Street but colloquially known as Commodore Street, after a cinema that was demolished decades ago (a hotel bearing that name now stands in its place). A major intersection on the edges of the city is known simply as Chevrolet, after a long-gone car factory. The Cola roundabout at the city's southern edge got its name from a factory that is no longer there either. You won't find the names on any official maps or street signs – these are our "phantom landmarks". Dissemination of information by the Ministry of Public Works, in charge of signage, leaves much to be desired and so directions are based upon what is next to a place or what used to be next to a place. People you ask for directions often confuse street names with neighbourhood names, and main-road names can become the name of their side streets as well.

> "Rapid changes in the urban landscape have led to directions that rely on the collective memory of residents"

So while it's fine for Beirut's residents to go about their daily lives, all knowing which direction they're heading, using street names to find your way around as a newcomer doesn't really work. That's why I developed the mapping company Zawarib, to create a sort of visual dictionary that bridges popular navigation traditions and the official addressing system. It lists official street and area names alongside the names of nearby landmarks – whether still standing or echoes of the past – that are still referenced by residents. The system was developed over many years, using satellite imagery for street layout and land use, as well as on-the-ground research into what the inhabitants of each neighbourhood employ for navigational guidance. Mostly it involved me walking the city street by street and alley by alley.

The result is like a series of love letters to a city full of charm and contrast, a city that I am proud to call home. It's a city that I can lose myself in – in a good way. — (M)

Names of the game
—
01 Ras Beirut
Located at, and literally meaning, the "tip of Beirut".
02 Accaoui Street
Named after a long-gone tram stop at the bottom of the road.
03 Fig tree (Tineh)
An area of the city, reflecting its lush surroundings before urban development.

ABOUT THE WRITER: Born in Beirut, Bahi Ghubril now divides his time between here and London. An engineer, traveller and entrepreneur, he is a keen explorer of urban communities.

ESSAY 05
Mixing it up
Lebanese cuisine

———

Meals in this slice of the Mediterranean are about more than just mezze and differ greatly depending on whether they're served in public or cooked at home.

by Kamal Mouzawak, writer and restaurateur

Broadly speaking, Lebanese food can be divided into two very distinct parts: public cuisine – found in restaurants and plied by street stands – and private cuisine, eaten at home. Most foreigners' only experience of Lebanese food is the former – or, more specifically, mezze.

This sacred procession starts with tabbouleh and *fattoush* and is followed by a selection of cold mezze: small dishes of thyme salad, hummus, *moutabal* (also known as baba ganoush) and white-bean salad. These are by no means appetisers because the meal is not built of standard courses of appetisers and mains. Instead they're a succession of different small plates. Next come the raw fillets of meat known as kibbeh, followed by the hot mezze of fried potato with coriander, fried kibbeh, *fatayer* (pastry stuffed with spinach or meat) and, to finish, skewers of barbequed meat or chicken known as *kafta*.

Akl el beit (home cuisine) is a world away from the dishes served in the public sphere. A lunch at home is never mezze.

Some of the mezze favourites may appear on the table but they will be served differently – mainly singularly and in larger portions. A meal at home consists of typical regional dishes and traditional recipes such as slow-cooked stews.

Home cuisine is more closely tied to the land and can be further broken down into two main divisions: an urban cuisine featuring abundant ingredients and sophisticated techniques; and

"Both urban and rural cuisines are deeply rooted in tradition and offer a taste of the land and the seasons"

a rural cuisine that's more rustic and based on the land's wealth, using common ingredients of wheat, *burghul* (bulgar), preserves, *keshek* (cereal made of *burghul* fermented with milk and yoghurt) and *awarma* (lamb confit). Both urban and rural cuisines are deeply rooted in tradition and offer a taste of the land and the seasons.

To me, cooking is the most vital and authentic way to perpetuate history, religions and expressions of oneself. It's a symbol of belonging, of community, of country – and for Lebanon it's a story of its people and geography.

Lebanon is petite in size and one of the smallest nations on the shore of the Mediterranean. Its rectangular patch is roughly divided into strips: a coastal plain, followed by the climbing ranges of Mount Lebanon, then a continental plateau and the Bekaa Valley, which preludes the deserts and steppes of Syria. Finally, the second mountain range of Anti Lebanon marks the border between Lebanon and Syria. It's a landscape that dictates the different climates, which in turn influence the types of agriculture, food production and, most importantly, the cuisine.

Coastal plains are lands of openness, trade and wealth. Most of Lebanon's cities are based along the coast and the cuisine here is unfalteringly rich, sophisticated and elaborate. Mountains, meanwhile, are lands of survival. The landscape is harsh and rocky. Winters are bitterly cold but dazzling; bright days define the summers. These conditions are favourable to growing produce that is then turned into modest but delightful home-cooked, almost survivalist-style meals.

But there are ways to turn this survival cookery into more contemporary dishes, by reinterpreting and mixing simple home food to create mezze that will fill the tables of feasts and celebrations. This approach to cooking seems popular across all the eastern Mediterranean countries.

When referencing food, all Lebanese describe the cuisine of our country in terms of who they are and where their roots lie. Beirut, Tripoli, Armenia, Aleppo, the coastal port towns, the soaring mountains, the inland expanses – for a country so small the diversity is astounding. Yet Lebanese cuisine and the variances between home and public dishes are just like all the things that distinguish and are created by this country: a mix of everything. — (M)

Top plates

01 Tabbouleh
A fresh and tasty mix of ingredients (like Lebanon itself).
02 'Manoushe'
The taste of breakfast from my village, with the smell of pine needles burning under the oven.
03 'Warraa arish'
Stuffed vine leaves, each perfectly rolled.

ABOUT THE WRITER: Kamal Mouzawak's career embraces food and travel writing, as well as cooking. He's the founder of Tawlet restaurant, Souk el Tayeb (Lebanon's first farmers' market) and Beit Projects.

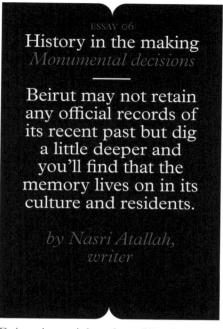

ESSAY 06
History in the making
Monumental decisions

___

Beirut may not retain any official records of its recent past but dig a little deeper and you'll find that the memory lives on in its culture and residents.

by Nasri Atallah, writer

Beirut is a tricky place. You have no doubt heard about its many contradictions, often expressed breathlessly, as if it were the only place on Earth that has them. East, West. Christian, Muslim. Historic, modern. Peace, war.

Sure, those juxtapositions exist and are often visceral. But the most striking aspect of the city – for me anyway – is that it's simultaneously heaving with history and devoid of any kind of memory; at least, not a formal one.

History seems to end after the withdrawal of French colonial troops – in the case of government-issue history books, quite literally. There are very few monuments to battles, heroes or victims, and those that exist have contested narratives.

In fact Lebanon is one of the only countries in the world to emerge from a protracted and bloody civil war without any kind of transitional justice movement, reconciliation council or monuments to show for it. At the conclusion of hostilities in 1990 the country was blanketed in collective amnesty, swiftly followed by collective amnesia. The warring factions swapped their militia fatigues for tailored suits and made their way to parliament.

Surely the fact that fighting stopped and peace prevailed should be enough for a city and country so severely battered by war – certainly any periods of peace in Lebanon are to be cherished. But the thing with memorials is that they indicate that something is over, that it has been meditated upon and will not repeat itself. They are national totems, at the base of which we bury painful moments and promise ourselves to reflect on them so that they may never creep up on us again. To not have any is worrisome.

This erasure of memory extends to the very fabric of the city: its squares, roads, buildings, architecture and archaeology. Their names, uses and narratives are constantly morphing, difficult to anchor. Just below the surface their contradictory histories simmer.

The city is a contested space and the memories invested in it are personal and conflicting. In the vacuum, some of the damaged buildings that survived the war

– and the reckless and unchecked demolition and reconstruction that followed – have themselves become makeshift memorials. Such buildings include the Holiday Inn by the Corniche (the scene of the blood-soaked Battle of the Hotels) and the so-called Egg in the Downtown area, originally a cinema and theatre and later a place to rave and recollect for a whole generation of 1990s kids trying to forget the stench of death that still shrouded the city. These sites have no plaques or inscriptions that would indicate any kind of collective meaning so it has been up to individuals to assign them whatever significance they see fit.

"Memorials indicate that something is over, that it has been meditated upon and will not repeat itself. They are national totems. To not have any is worrisome"

There are occasionally reasons to be hopeful. One such example is Beit Beirut, a new museum and cultural centre. Housed in the Barakat Building, a battle-worn architectural gem in the Ottoman revivalist style, it sits at a busy intersection on a street that used to be known as the Green Line. This demarcation zone between east and west emerged during the 1975 to 1990 civil war and was named after the vegetation sprouting in the land separating the opposing snipers.

For years the building had been one of those makeshift symbols of the war and threatened with demolition. But in 2007 the city's mayor confirmed that it would become a museum. The long, arduous decade from that announcement to its doors opening shows how difficult it can be to bring such a project to life in a city like Beirut. It's still unclear whether it will remain open permanently but it's worth attempting a visit regardless.

Of course, if you're up for a bit of digging, Lebanon's relationship to its past can be detected elsewhere. You can find it in Rabee Jaber's 2008 novel *Confessions*, which features roadblocks, death, kidnapping and a subterranean Beirut full of its undead souls. You can find it in Zena El Khalil's *Beirut, I Love You*, a poignant memoir of life during the 2006 war with Israel. You can find it in Maroun Baghdadi's 1982 film *Little Wars* and Ghassan Salhab's 1998 film *Beyrouth Fantome*. Any of these will provide you with a window into what the city looked and felt like in a way that perhaps no memorial or museum ever could. On a personal, possibly perverse level, I think my favourite version of Beirut is the one in Salhab's film, the one just emerging from war. Damaged but hopeful.

Above all, however, you will find the memory of Beirut in the voices of its inhabitants. If you cut through the universal exasperation at power cuts, water shortages and the inept political class, you will come across dozens of people who will happily share a meal and their stories. Of course, this means you will come away with a very personal sense of what the city's memories are, a path of individual histories representing the intersection of your own curiosity with the human fabric of the city.

No two visitors come away with the same understanding of Beirut's memory but, then again, no two visitors will come away with the same understanding of Beirut itself. There are no clear outlines for the first-time visitor to follow. You will have to carve out your own path. — (M)

Beirut novels
---
01 **'De Niro's Game'**
Two friends must choose between crime and a life in exile.
02 **'Gate of the Sun'**
A tale of displacement and hope.
03 **'Sitt Marie Rose'**
Based on the story of Marie Rose Boulos, who was executed by a Christian militia.

ABOUT THE WRITER: Nasri Atallah is a British-Lebanese writer and media entrepreneur. He is the author of both *Our Man in Beirut* and a forthcoming crime novel set in the city. He lives in London.

ESSAY 07

The kindness of strangers
Lebanese hospitality

———

Amid the exquisite palaces, lively party scene and tasty plates, it's the unrestrained generosity of the Lebanese that's truly going to stick with you when you bid Beirut farewell.

by Venetia Rainey,
Monocle

During your travels in Beirut there's one phrase you are bound to hear time and time again: *ahlan wa sahlan*. It means "welcome" but can be more literally translated as "you are among family, be at ease". It embodies a deeply ingrained spirit of hospitality.

This part of the world has an ancient nomadic culture of looking after a stranger who seeks shelter and, although it is no longer strictly adhered to, people across the region still place great value on the simple practice of accommodating guests in every way possible. Therefore, at the behest of tradition, foreigners are welcomed with unrivalled warmth, ranging from endless offerings of food and drink to the genuine, sometimes superfluous generosity that marks every interaction.

While living in Beirut it was impossible for me to enter or leave my first-floor apartment without the two people living downstairs inviting me in for some tea or a bite to eat. At first, to someone trained in the big-city western art of avoiding any

meaningful or prolonged interaction with neighbours, this felt like an imposition. But with time I grew to love it – this was my neighbours' way of making me feel at home.

This approach to complete strangers was something I often experienced while out reporting. No matter how pressed someone was they would always make time to show me the way to a hard-to-find address or help track down the phone number of a tricksy contact. When I asked a Palestinian man I had only just met in a run-down camp in south Lebanon where I could buy a packet of crisps, he insisted I have lunch with his family and threw me an impromptu falafel feast.

I was also regularly struck by the way in which those who had so little to call their own would go out of their way to make me feel part of the family. One example in particular sticks in my mind. I was at a makeshift camp in the Bekaa Valley in the middle of winter, interviewing Syrian refugees. It had snowed heavily and was bitterly cold so one woman invited me into her home for a chat. It was a small single room made of concrete breeze blocks and we kept our coats on inside. As she told me how she was struggling to get by she plied me with cardamom-laced coffee and biscuits – it was an instinctive desire to host that most would have forgiven her for skipping given the circumstances.

This is an attitude that's by no means limited to the man or woman in the street: it also extends into the realm of politics. Up in the mountainous Chouf region, residents descend weekly upon the magnificent personal home of the Jumblatts, the Lebanese Druze political dynasty behind the country's Progressive Socialist party. All are welcome to attend this open-house whether they come to voice a complaint, ask for a job or simply say hello.

"With Arab hospitality you need to modestly let your guest feel as if he or she is the actual owner of the house so they can feel at home," says Teymour Jumblatt, the son of veteran politician Walid Jumblatt. "One should always keep in mind that people tend to form great bonds over food and drink – breaking bread is key.

"Arab hospitality is not a spectator sport. The best way to explain it is to actually practise it and let the people around you feel it," he adds. "Moukhtara Palace has been dubbed the House of the People and I would like to keep it as such."

For Jumblatt's father, who has been running the event for decades, it's almost an ancient rite. "Traditionally, when you knock on the door and you present yourself, I have to greet you and accommodate you or any guest for three days," he says.

Of course, we shouldn't paint too rosy a picture of the tradition because this sense of hospitality doesn't always extend to other religions, nationalities or social classes. Sectarianism in particular is an enormous problem in Lebanon, something that dates back to before the war and permeates every institution in the country.

Racism too is a big issue, particularly with regards to migrant workers, who are legally no better than slaves and are socially regarded by many as members of an underclass. The country hosts more than a million Syrian refugees – that's a staggering number when you consider its population is just four million – but many of them face discrimination on a daily basis. It's also home to just under half a million Palestinians, most of whom were born in the country but are nonetheless impoverished, unable to acquire Lebanese nationality and banned from earning a living in many professions.

That aside, as a visitor to this country you will likely be blown away by the generosity you find extended to you by total strangers. Whether it's time, food or energy, the people here share what they have without explicitly expecting anything in return. It's this instinctive trust in human nature – trust that, if they needed it, you would return their kindness – that makes the Lebanese some of the most genuinely hospitable people on the planet. — (M)

> *"People share what they have without explicitly expecting anything in return. It is an instinctive trust in human nature – trust that if they needed it, you would return their kindness"*

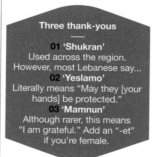

Three thank-yous

01 'Shukran'
Used across the region. However, most Lebanese say...
02 'Yeslamo'
Literally means "May they [your hands] be protected."
03 'Mamnun'
Although rarer, this means "I am grateful." Add an "-et" if you're female.

ABOUT THE WRITER: Venetia Rainey is MONOCLE's former Beirut correspondent. She lived there for four years and makes sure she grabs a cup of tea with her old neighbours every time she's back. She now reports for MONOCLE from Amsterdam.

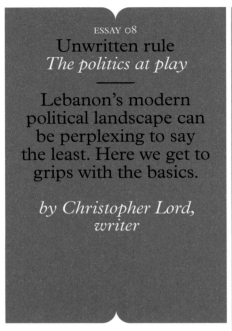

ESSAY 08
Unwritten rule
The politics at play

———

Lebanon's modern political landscape can be perplexing to say the least. Here we get to grips with the basics.

by Christopher Lord,
writer

Abdallah Farah was a Lebanese photographer who, in 1968, was hired to snap Beirut for a series of postcards. His lens captured the frivolity of the sunny Corniche, the optimistic high-rises and tended beachfronts. Collectively his images were a picture-postcard idea of Beirut as a cosmopolitan Mediterranean Riviera.

But when civil war broke out in 1975, Farah, like other Lebanese, was forced inside his home. Yet during the 15-year conflict the photographer did his best to document the changing city. As gunfights were reported on the radio and buildings were bombed, he burnt off parts of his negatives to reflect the devastation. Those negatives became one man's personal record of the war.

But Farah and his archive of scarred images is a fiction. He is the creation of two of Lebanon's most celebrated contemporary artists, Joana Hadjithomas and Khalil Joreige, and part of their project *Wonder Beirut*, which has been exhibited extensively since it was started in 1997.

The point of the work is that Lebanese history, especially that of the 15-year civil war, is personal to every Lebanese person.

There's no concrete narrative of exactly how the war unfolded and nor is there a museum about it in the city. So it's worth reading up a little about Lebanon and its tumultuous 20th century before you visit.

Like much of the eastern Mediterranean, Lebanon has long been a diverse place: Maronite Catholics, Sunni and Shia Muslims, Druze, Jews and various orthodoxies all lived alongside one another. It was ruled for 400 years by Ottoman Turks, and the bullet-riddled Martyrs' Monument in the centre of Beirut was built in the name of those hanged for agitating for independence.

When the empire was defeated at the end of the First World War, control of the country shifted to France before Lebanon got its independence in 1943. That year, however, a key component of what has shaped the country's history was created: the National Pact. This decreed that the president of the country must be Maronite Christian, the prime minister a Sunni Muslim, the speaker of parliament a Shia, and the deputy speaker Greek Orthodox. This balancing act between the communities still exists today and the structure of politics remains intact. For such a defining agreement, however, the National Pact was never written down.

> *"Knowing about Lebanon and its 20th century is, in some way, to understand the divisions that shape the modern Middle East"*

The UN partition plan of Palestine and the creation of the state of Israel in 1948 saw an influx of refugees, shifting the demographics of Lebanese society as more Sunni and Shia Palestinians fled to the country. Yet the National Pact still stipulated a Maronite Christian should be head of state.

Eventually this verbal agreement between the various sects in Lebanon led to tension. Society became more polarised along sectarian lines and armed factions were pitted against each other. By the time war broke out in 1975 it was a war of militias, with Israel backing the Maronite Christian "Phalange" groups and Iran backing the Shia militias who would become the Hezbollah that exists today.

The war was long and torrid. It was an urban civilian war, punctuated by mass displacement, an Israeli invasion and massacres that are remembered among the darkest moments in Middle Eastern history. Therefore the full story is yet to be agreed upon even inside Lebanon.

Somehow, however, the National Pact survived. That unwritten agreement from 1943 continues to dictate the structure of Lebanese politics and the religious beliefs of those who hold high office.

It's a symbol of the curious postwar state that Lebanon has been in since the end of the war. Like Abdallah Farah and his warped negatives, everyone has their own story of how Lebanon got to where it is today. Theirs are personal, private histories that are yet to be properly set in stone. — (M)

**Influential
Lebanese creatives**
—
01 Lawrence Abu Hamdan
Explores how sound intersects
with politics.
02 Marwa Arsanios
Film director who covered
Beirut's rubbish crisis.
03 Tony Chakar
Writes about Beirut's art
and architecture.

ABOUT THE WRITER: Christopher Lord is MONOCLE's former features editor. Previously based in the Middle East for eight years, he has watched the sun come up over Beirut more times than he cares to remember.

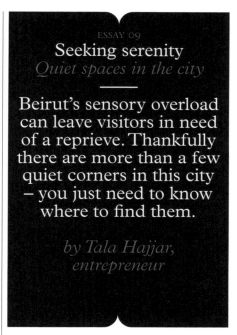

ESSAY 09
Seeking serenity
Quiet spaces in the city
—
Beirut's sensory overload can leave visitors in need of a reprieve. Thankfully there are more than a few quiet corners in this city – you just need to know where to find them.

*by Tala Hajjar,
entrepreneur*

The moment you land in Beirut it can feel as if you've toppled into an urban set of *Alice in Wonderland*. The scenery, colours, smells and certainly the tastes of the city (and the cacophony of it all) can hypnotise you.

Although this enchanting mix is helplessly addictive it can also be overwhelming. So it's only natural that, at times, visitors might feel in need of a moment or two of reprieve. But where to find such a thing in a city lacking in green spaces?

Make a beeline for the Ein el Mraysseh district and begin your decompression at the Corniche or, more specifically, under the unmistakable Ficus Nitida tree. This particular species was the plant of choice in the golden 1960s. Don't stop there: venture a little further west to soak up more of this coastal strip. Preferably this wander is accompanied by some smooth jazz but don't worry if you've forgotten your headphones: there's a chorus of tunes sounding from the speakers of parked cars or the boom boxes of families and friends gathered here. Stay a while, taking in this landscape and its carnival of people who are jogging, fishing, chatting, flirting and posing against the backdrop of the Mediterranean's dark-blue hues.

If it's a long and lazy meal you're chasing, nowhere beats Casablanca (*see page 32*). A succulent lunch of Asian-fusion food is best paired with the house special: a lychee martini. Casablanca is more than a restaurant to us Beirutis. It's an institution where we go to recover from a Saturday night on the tiles, usually opting for the simple but scrumptious eggs Benedict. We've also developed a relationship with each member of staff, including the incredible owners Johnny and Cyn Farah.

Another great little retreat is restaurant Gruen. Located at the foot of the Gefinor Center (one of Beirut's architectural landmarks), it's ideal for afternoon tea. Normally one of the busiest areas on weekdays, it's as silent as a shadow come Sunday. Recline in the charming interior and reflect on the bustling Beirut that lies just beyond its glass doors.

"Take in this landscape and its carnival of people who are jogging, fishing, chatting and flirting"

Last but certainly not least is the trophy: the AUB campus (*see pages 87 and 118*). The botany and history of the grounds offer enough intrigue to keep you occupied for hours, or you can simply get lost and sit by a sprawling tree. Breathe in the crisp air and absorb the vistas from the benches. This campus has an infectious and calming power.

In the words of the White Rabbit from *Alice in Wonderland*, "The hurrier I go, the behinder I get." Allowing for a change in pace is imperative in Beirut, if only so you wake up refreshed and ready for another day of adventures. — (M)

Top jazz spots
—
01 **Dragonfly, Gemmayzeh**
Dim lighting, sharp cocktails and old-school jazz.
02 **Blue Note Café, Hamra**
The city's best address for jazz and blues.
03 **Salon Beyrouth, Clemenceau**
Jazz-era decor and tunes, plus plenty of whiskey.

ABOUT THE WRITER: With previous experience in fashion marketing, today Tala Hajjar works mostly with fashion designer Rabih Kayrouz. Together the pair co-founded the non-profit design incubator Starch Foundation in 2008.

ESSAY 10

Raising the bar
Liquid Lebanon

With myriad wineries, a longstanding love affair with beer and, of course, a healthy production line of arak, Lebanon offers plenty of opportunities to raise a glass.

*by Alex Rowell,
writer*

"When abroad you drink and eat as the locals do, or there seems not much point in going," wrote the late Kingsley Amis in his invaluable tome of wisdom, *Everyday Drinking*. Lebanon is justly renowned for the making of merry with cutlery and glassware and you are strongly encouraged to branch out from the "usual" you order from the pub chain back home.

Drinks-wise the country produces its own beer, wine and a grape-and-aniseed distillate called arak – and all three to an admirable and ever-improving standard. What more agreeable way to acclimatise and get to know the place – the very land itself – than to taste the fruits of its soil?

Wine has been made in Lebanon for millennia. The ancient Phoenician inhabitants of the coast not only drank but exported it around the Mediterranean as far as Spain and modern Tunisia. A magnificently well-preserved Temple of Bacchus in the eastern town of Baalbeck, in the vine-rich plains of the Bekaa Valley, attests to the enthusiasm felt for the wine

deity in Roman times. One of the earliest poets of the Arabic language, the pre-Islamic Amr ibn Kulthum from Iraq, spoke wistfully of drinking "many a glass" in the same town.

The serious oenophile, then, is going to want to plan a trip to the Bekaa, where about half of the country's 50-odd producers are found. Ksara and Kefraya are the largest and perhaps most tourist-convenient wineries to visit, though the smaller, more intimate Château Saint Thomas offers guests a broader and, to my mind, better range of actual wine. The latter is also the first to have made a white wine exclusively from an indigenous grape variety: the light and citric obeidy.

If you're unable to leave the city, the ideal place to try these and many other local wines (and yes, plenty of excellent European and New World varieties) is the relaxed and radically affordable new Cantina Sociale, off Sassine Square. Pour yourself a glass from one of its self-service dispenser machines or, better yet, pluck one of its 370-plus bottles off the shelves and pop it open.

"The serious oenophile is going to want to plan a trip to the Bekaa, where about half of the country's 50-odd producers are found"

Beer, too, boasts a lengthy pedigree in the country, as in the neighbourhood at large. The staple tipple of both the ancient Egyptians and the Sumerians (for whom Ninkasi was its patron goddess), it's also known to have been made closer to home in Syria's Ebla (now Tell Mardikh, Idlib Province) in the third millennium BC, from where it was likely distributed to the Lebanese territories under Ebla's rule. At any rate, modern Lebanese beer began in 1933 with Almaza (The Diamond), whose pilsner remains the ubiquitous face of the industry to this day – though aficionados often prefer the ales of microbrewer rival 961. If you can, drive up the coast to

Batroun, where the Colonel Craft Brewery sits right on the beach. To imbibe a flight or two of its more than 10 draughts – ranging from passion fruit infusion through India pale ales to stouts – and then stumble into the Mediterranean can be a profitable way to spend an afternoon.

For those confined to the capital, acquiring an Almaza involves no more than a walk to the nearest corner shop. But craft concoctions are slightly harder to come by. Badaro's Brew inc has an on-site microbrewery, producing up to seven draughts, including a pleasantly heady, hoppy IPA and a sweet, nutty porter. Elsewhere, as well as serving the best French press in town, Kalei Coffee Co in Mar Mikhael is one of relatively few establishments to stock Colonel, along with an extensive range of imports. On top of that, in-house shop The Carton does a side in independent small-batch arak.

As much as wine and beer can jostle for its title, it's still this invigorating distillation – roughly akin to Greek ouzo, Turkish raki, French pastis – that is the one true *sine qua non* of the traditional Lebanese lunch and dinner table. Stronger than claret but milder than a glass of Scotch, its mysterious powers include (but are not limited to) the whetting of the appetite, the cleansing of the palate, the aiding of digestion and, of course, the enlivening of conversation.

While brands do exist, it's widely agreed that the best stuff is the unbranded rural moonshine, triple-distilled each year by villagers according to meticulous age-old custom, the copper stills fired by vine-wood embers and the aniseed sourced specifically from the Syrian village of Hineh. For those of us without a mountain-dwelling Lebanese cousin to arrange delivery, Anise bar in Mar Mikhael offers a fix. Alongside the superb collection of spirits populating its shelves (Anise happens to be one of Beirut's greatest cocktail bars) stands a row of 12 bottles of transparent liquid. Each is a village-made arak procured from regions spanning the length of the country, from Akkar on the northern border to Rmeish at the extreme south. Co-owner and head barman Hisham al-Hussein says his favourite comes from the Bekaa Valley's Furzul, describing it fondly as "smooth, a little sweet, with not too much anise".

Rolling its zesty, vivifying solution around the gums, you begin to understand why the laureate of 9th-century Baghdad bacchanalia, Abu Nuwas, implored his friends: "Should I die on Syria's land, don't leave me far from al-Furzul." — (M)

Essential Lebanese vocabulary
——
01 Beer
Bira – who said Arabic was hard?
02 Wine
Nbeed, followed by *ahmar* for red and *abyad* for white.
03 Cheers!
Késak if addressing a man, *késik* for a woman and *késkon* for a group.

ABOUT THE WRITER: Alex Rowell is a Beirut-based journalist and editor, and author of *Vintage Humour: The Islamic Wine Poetry of Abu Nuwas*.

Culture
—— Against
the odds

Nowhere is the Lebanese spirit of perseverance encapsulated so poetically as in its cultural cache. Modern Beirut was razed by the 1975 to 1990 civil war only to bounce back by installing galleries in bomb shelters *(see page 92)* as the dust settled.

The city's cultural capital took shape in the wake of the conflict and has been growing ever since, despite simmering tensions and a lack of government arts funding. Further boosts came with the founding of Beirut Art Fair in 2010, Beirut Design Week in 2012 and the reopening of the Sursock Museum in 2015 following its seven-year renovation. With the region regalvanised, new galleries opened apace – and with a raft of ambitious projects underway and museums set to open in the next few years *(see page 88)*, the boom looks no closer to ending.

Art aside, the Lebanese capital hosts screenings, concerts, cabaret and everything else you'd expect from a major metropolis, despite its diminutive size. With all that culture condensed into such a small area, there's never been a better time to visit this dynamic and ever-changing city.

①
National Museum of Beirut, Mathaf
Set in stone

Emir Maurice Chehab was a quick thinker. In 1982, after the National Museum of Beirut had already closed its doors and in the midst of the city's worsening 15-year civil war, its first director sealed its most important archaeological artefacts in concrete to prevent them from being looted or destroyed. They wouldn't be unearthed until 1997.

Today, after years of renovations, the museum is open once more. Inside you'll find marble sarcophagi from the 2nd century alongside ancient Egyptian sculptures inscribed with hieroglyphics, as well as assorted Bronze Age, Iron Age, Hellenistic, Roman and Byzantine objects. With the war over, all that's left are memories and scars – and some of the museum's are very visible. The "Mosaic of the Good Shepherd", a vast wall-mounted artwork dating from the 5th century, still bears a hole made by a sniper seeking a convenient lookout point.
Museum Street
+961 (0)1 426 703
beirutnationalmuseum.com

2
Nicolas Ibrahim Sursock
Museum, Sursock
Open house

Built as a villa for aristocrat and
art-lover Nicolas Sursock in
1912, this Venetian-Ottoman-
style building was turned into
a museum following his death
and today exhibits a varied
collection of contemporary and
modern art. The museum has
undergone multiple renovations
and is now five times bigger
than it was at the time of its
1961 opening. But throughout
its several facelifts there has
been one constant: Sursock's
study has been left untouched,
with its 19th-century furniture,
Islamic tiles and wood-panelled
walls all on display.

Spread across the museum
you'll find more than 800 works
by artists such as Omar Onsi,
Yvette Achkar, Aref el Rayess
and Ali Cherri. Also worth
checking out are the library
and the auditorium.
*Greek Orthodox
Archbishopric Street
+961 (0)1 202 001
sursock.museum*

③
The AUB Archaeological Museum, Hamra
Pulling teeth

Set on the American University of Beirut's (AUB) campus and founded in 1868, this is one of the oldest museums in the Near East. Its artefacts come from Lebanon, Syria, Palestine, Egypt, Iraq and Iran and date from the Early Stone Age through to the Islamic Golden Age.

Alongside Paleolithic flint tools and Phoenician glassware, the most jaw-dropping exhibit is just that: a jaw. The Ford mandible dates from the 5th century BC and features six loose teeth bound in golden wire to prevent them from falling out. It's the earliest example of dentistry in the known world – and a great reminder to brush twice a day.
Bliss Street
+961 (0)1 759 665
aub.edu.lb/museum_archeo

④
Dar El-Nimer, Clemenceau
History lesson

Palestinian art collector Rami El-Nimer founded this museum in 2015. It resides in a 1930s Le Corbusier-inspired building and is dedicated to historical, modern and contemporary cultural productions from Palestine, the Levant and beyond.

Rami's collection documents 10 centuries of civilisation and features manuscripts, armour and more, all of which are employed to help deconstruct damaging clichés that dog the Middle East. Whether it's an exhibition on Arabic calligraphy, Syrian sculpture or Palestinian embroidery, every item on display at Dar El-Nimer makes a statement.
Villa Salem, America Street
+961 (0)1 367 013
darelnimer.org

⑤
Mim Museum, Sodeco
Hidden gem

From tanzanite's iridescent hues to the implausible angles of Australia's crimson crocoite, you'd be forgiven for thinking that the Mim's contents were mined from some distant alien planet. In fact, they were all formed right here on Earth.

Hidden beyond the entrance of the Saint Joseph University building, the mineral museum features more than 1,800 geological wonders from some 70 countries. The collection sees minerals arranged by their chemical classification, alongside thematic presentations. To say that the museum is made up of natural masterpieces would be an understatement: high-quality materials were used in its very construction, from its quartzite walls to its labradorite-paved entrance. We could say more but by now the reasons for visiting the Mim should be crystal clear.
Université Saint Joseph Campus de L'innovation et du Sport (CIS)
+961 (0)1 421 672

(6)
Aïshti Foundation, Antelias
Lap of luxury

Tony Salamé is the founder of Lebanese luxury retailer Aïshti and an avid collector of contemporary art. His inventory grew to such proportions over the past decade that he had an entire museum constructed just to contain it. The result, opened in 2015, is a striking David Adjaye-designed building that's part high-end shopping centre, part art gallery, all dizzying grandeur.

Set across four floors – two of which are double-height – each exhibition sees the gallery play host to about a tenth of Salamé's 2,000-piece collection. If you get tired of the stunning contemporary art (as if), head to the ground floor and through the Urban Retreat Café to the rear of the building, where permanent pieces sit on the banks of the Mediterranean and the city glistens in the distance.
Aïshti Building,
Seaside Road
+961 (0)1 991 111
aishtifoundation.com

In the works

Construction is abundant here and anyone with cash can tear down a traditional Lebanese home and erect an office tower in its place. Thankfully there are a few Beiruti benefactors who are putting their fortunes to better use. Here are some of the city's best upcoming art institutions.

01 Beirut City Museum: Martyrs' Square will soon be home to an arresting glass cube that will invite visitors to explore the city's archaeological heritage, ancient past and recent history.
02 Beirut Museum of Art: Set to host an exhibition featuring 1,000 works from more than 450 Lebanese artists, all eyes will be on the Bema when it opens in 2020 – and not just because of the 120-metre-tall tower at the museum's core.
03 The Museum of Arab Art: This free-to-enter museum will be the city's biggest art institution when it opens in 2020 and will house the more than 4,000 pieces of modern and contemporary art that make up the Dalloul family's collection.

Pray tell
———

Hidden beneath the Saint George Greek Orthodox Cathedral is an archaeological crypt museum that displays ancient artefacts found during excavations of the vicinity in 1994. Expect to see everything from smoking pipes and pottery to arrowheads and amulets.

Public galleries
Show time

①

Beirut Art Center,
Palais De Justice
Out of the ordinary

Beirut Art Center has been one
of the cornerstones of the city's
cultural scene since opening
in 2009. Far removed from hip
Hamra and Gemmayzeh, the
gallery sits on the edge of town
in an area that has so far
avoided gentrification. Artistic
director Marie Muracciole,
though, sees its out-of-the-way
position as a positive: "People
come here on purpose."

The non-profit
institution's ambitious remit
sees it supporting regional
contemporary artists and,
through its six annual
experimental-art shows,
shining a light on topics and
places that are sorely absent
in Lebanese cultural media.
13 Jisr El Wati, Street 97
+961 (0)1 397 018
beirutartcenter.org

②

Station, Palais De Justice
Action stations

Just an olive's toss from Beirut
Art Center, Station serves
as a platform for artists and
curators and is an important
fixture of the city's art and
music scenes. Founded in 2013,
its large space is dedicated to
visual, performing and digital
arts and its interdisciplinary
programme is inspired by the
city's cultural happenings. With
bold and progressive exhibitions
alongside workshops, concerts,
performances and more, as well
as the occasional craft market,
it's a good idea to keep an eye
on the Station schedule while
you're in town.
Street 90
+961 (0)71 684 218
stationbeirut.com

Home team

01 Beirut Art Residency, Gemmayzeh: This non-profit foundation welcomes artists from all disciplines and its residency programme, which culminates in a public exhibition, is an important stepping stone for emerging artists. Alongside its live-work space, it also operates La Vitrine. This tiny space is designed to be viewed from the outside rather than entered. Through its bimonthly exhibits it prompts the people of Gemmayzeh to stop and focus on something other than the busy streets.
beirutartresidency.com

02 Mansion, Patrakieh: Abandoned during the 15-year civil war, this grand 1930s villa in the city centre was left empty until 2012, when some savvy creatives rescued the space from obscurity. Today Mansion is home to 10 studios and hosts performances, screenings and exhibitions.
mansion-blatt.blogspot. co.uk

03 House of Today, Bab Idriss: Established by Cherine Magrabi Tayeb in 2012, House of Today acts as a platform for emerging Lebanese designers. Alongside its scholarship programme and support of creative initiatives, the non-profit hosts exhibitions, lectures and workshops, as well as its biennale, which showcases the collaboration between experts and fledgling designers under a unified theme.
houseoftoday.com

③
Ashkal Alwan, Palais De Justice
Life in plastic

Ashkal Alwan, the Lebanese Association for Plastic Arts, is a large communal space that welcomes creatives who are free to work, research and peruse its library. Meanwhile, talks, screenings and concerts keep artistic types on their toes and spark conversation between curators, artists, photographers and philosophers. With both its residency and home workspace programmes, the non-profit organisation is a major contributor to Arab art. In a city that has limited public space, this cultural playground is an invaluable resource for residents.
Building 110, Street 90
+961 (0)1 423 879
ashkalalwan.org

Drawing Objects
Sigve Knutson

①
Carwan Gallery, Karantina
First-rate design

Founded by architects Nicolas
Bellavance-Lecompte and
Pascale Wakim, Carwan was the
Middle East's first contemporary
design gallery. What began as a
pop-up in 2010 has since taken
up residence in D-Beirut, a
1960s factory building now
home to a prime creative space.

Today, Carwan's showroom
is a place where architecture,
art and design overlap. The
gallery exhibits limited-edition
objects, such as the wood-clay
furniture of Norway's Sigve
Knutson and the playful
tableware of Lebanese designer
Carlo Massoud. It encourages
designers to meld the practices
of western design with the
traditional techniques of the
East and its name reflects that:
Carwan comes from the Arabic
caravanserai, a place where
caravans would stop to rest on
long trade routes.
D-Beirut Building,
Seaside Road
+961 (0)3 686 089
carwangallery.com

② Saleh Barakat Gallery, Clemenceau
Anniversary art

Artists were prolific during Lebanon's 15-year civil war but had nowhere to showcase their work. That all changed in 1991 when Saleh Barakat opened Agial. Creatives finally had a platform even if, due to the city's volatility, Barakat's insurers insisted that their work be displayed in the modest space's underground bomb shelter – safety first.

Twenty-five years later Barakat opened his eponymous gallery to celebrate Agial's 25th anniversary. The gallery focuses on modern and contemporary Lebanese and Levantine art and works hard to strip away the pretense present in many artistic environments; you'll find no hifalutin discourse here. Instead expect barbed-wire sculptures by Palestinian artist Abdul Rahman Katanani alongside works by the likes of landscape artist Daniele Genadry and Lebanese abstract pioneer Saloua Raouda Choucain.
Justinian Street
+961 (0)1 365 615
salehbarakatgallery.com

③ Galerie Tanit, Mar Mikhael
Big-name art

Tanit may be a bastion of Beirut's art scene but its roots lie in the West. The gallery was founded by Naila Kettaneh-Kunigk and her husband in Munich in 1972 but, sensing artistic rumblings in the Middle East, she opened a space here in 2007.

From its purpose-built home, Tanit works with international artists as well as those from the Arab world, including David Kramer and Iranian painter Shirin Ettehadieh. The gallery has also collaborated with the likes of Jeff Koons. In fact, as far as the artists who have worked with Tanit go, Kettaneh-Kunigk says: "Name them, they've been here."
East Village Building,
Armenia Street
+961 (0)1 562 812
galerietanit.com

Surely this is enough to get me exhibited

④

Marfa', Port District
Port of call

You'll find Marfa' not in Beirut's
artistic district Gemmayzeh but
at the very forefront of the city
– and there's a good reason for
that. This portside showroom
embraces the connotations that
come with its location: the
incomings, the outgoings and
the exchange of goods and ideas.
 The same concepts run
through its programme. Marfa'
works with emerging and
mid-career artists from the
region to put on narrative-led
exhibitions. From Lamia
Joreige's explorations of the
city's landscape to Ahmad
Ghossein's questions about land
and space, the gallery provides
insight into the region's past,
present and future.
*Al Marfa'a, off Charles
Helou Avenue
+961 (0)1 571 636
marfaprojects.com*

⑤

Joy Mardini Design Gallery, Gemmayzeh
Making it work

Prior to the advent of Joy
Mardini's gallery in 2011 there
were few shops in the city in
which Lebanese designers
could sell their wares. Today the
space allows them to display
their objects – practical pieces
such as Carla Baz's brushed-
brass lamps and Karim Chaya's
rocking chairs – on an
international scale.
 Across its four annual
exhibitions the showroom
is stocked with functioning
products in shows bound by
such varied themes as 1920s
prohibition and Fibonacci's
golden ratio. Designers
are encouraged to adopt
techniques and materials
typical to the Middle East.
*Najem Building, Gouraud Street
+961 (0)1 443 263
jmdesigngallery.com*

⑥

The AUB Art Gallery, Ein el Mraysseh
Learn your lesson

Set among the stray cats and
sprawling banyan trees of its
seaside campus, the American
University of Beirut plays an
active role in promoting fine
and contemporary art in the
region. Although currently
composed of two spaces – one
dedicated to modern Middle
Eastern art and the other to
international contemporary
pieces – the plan is to unite
them across two floors of the
campus's Mary Dodge Hall by
late 2018. For now the galleries
host four annual shows
alongside workshops, all of
which are tied into the
university's curriculum, making
these the perfect places in
which to brush up on your art
history. Be sure to take notes.
*+961 (0)1 350 000
aub.edu.lb/art_galleries*

⑦

Galerie Janine Rubeiz, Raoucheh
In memoriam

Janine Rubeiz was a shining light
in Lebanese art: she founded
Dar El Fan, one of the country's
first cultural centres, in 1967.
Though it was destroyed by
militias less than a decade later,
across its short tenure the centre
hosted 90 exhibitions, 60 poetry
nights, 150 film screenings and
more than 240 conferences.
 The Rubeiz legacy lives on
in this gallery, founded by her
daughter Nadine Begdache in
1993, a year after her mother's
passing. With a collection of
more than 900 contemporary
and modern artwork from
Lebanese and Arab artists, the
gallery more than holds its own
on Beirut's booming art scene.
*Majdalani Building (Bank Audi),
Charles de Gaulle Avenue
+961 (0)1 868 290
galeriejaninerubeiz.com*

①

Dar al-Mussawir, Clemenceau
Snap to it

Meaning "House of the Photographer" in Arabic, Dar al-Mussawir is a hub for shutterbugs. Set above Dar Bistro & Books *(see page 61)* and founded by photojournalist Ramzi Haidar in 2010, the institution offers training programmes and equipment hire, while also hosting exhibitions and lectures. It also boasts one of the city's few fully functioning darkrooms and an impressive collection of cameras, some of which date back to the 1800s.

Dar al-Mussawir is an extension of Haidar's work. As well as covering international crises he is the founder of Zakira, a non-profit dedicated to civic photography. Zakira works with marginalised communities such as prisoners, Palestinian refugees and the stateless, and much of its work appears here.
Alley 83, off Roma Street
+961 (0)1 373 347
daralmussawir.org

⑧

Sfeir-Semler Gallery, Karantina
Get lost

Andrée Sfeir-Semler founded her eponymous gallery in Kiel in 1985 and her Beirut space opened 20 years later in the midst of Lebanon's artistic awakening. Soon after that it had an awakening of its own: the gallery began by showing modernist art but when it started working with artists from the region its programme became more contemporary.

With more than 34 artists on its roster, including Walid Raad and Wael Shawky, the gallery allows visitors to see the city's minute details from unlikely perspectives. It's easy to get lost in Sfeir-Semler Gallery – and not just because it's one of the biggest commercial galleries in the Arab world.
Tannous Building
+961 (0)1 566 550
sfeir-semler.com

And on your right, you have...

2
Arab Image Foundation,
Gemmayzeh
Photo op

Want to see whirling dervishes
from the 1880s? Or wedding
photos from 1960s Alexandria?
How about an oiled-up wrestler
from 1940s Aleppo? Then the
Arab Image Foundation is a
must-visit. The non-profit is
dedicated to the collection and
preservation of photography
from the Arab world. Its archive
features about 600,000 objects
from 10 countries, most of
which are yet to be digitised
and processed.

The images range from
amateur snapshots to the works
of well-known Armenian-
Egyptian photographer Van
Leo. But far from being
merely a bank of images,
the foundation is a sharing
platform with public events
taking place across the city. As
well as a library of more than
2,500 publications and films,
visitors can browse about
45,000 processed images and
in doing so learn that the
history of Arab photography is
anything but black and white.
Zoghbi Building,
337 Gouraud Street
+961 (0)1 569 373
fai.org.lb

Live venues
Beat perfect

①
Blue Note Café, Hamra
All that jazz

Don't be fooled by its
unassuming appearance; this
down-to-earth joint will have
you up on your feet come
nightfall. A humble café by day,
Blue Note kicks out the jams
when the sun goes down as
renowned jazz, blues, funk and
traditional Arabic and Oriental
musicians take to the stage
to get people moving.

Dancing the night away
will have you working up an
appetite and thankfully Blue
Note can cater to those needs
too: the kitchen turns out
Levantine cuisine until late to
keep energies high. Maintain
your stamina with some
homemade *shanklish* –
Lebanese cheese made from
cow or sheep's milk and spiced
with zaatar – and a glass of
local wine. Evenings here boast
an electric atmosphere; it's
best to book in advance as the
small space gets busy fast.
Makhoul Street
+961 (0)1 743 857
bluenotecafe.com

*Now I'm
feeling
funky*

❷

Metro al Madina, Hamra
Take the stage

This independent theatre opened with a New Year's Eve show in 2012 and – with a diverse programme of concerts, musicals and lively cabaret – its momentum hasn't slowed since. The colourful space counts both 18-year-olds and 80-year-olds among its regulars, who come to see nightly shows that range from theatre to pop and rock music.

Egyptian cabaret Hishik Bishik has been running since 2013 and is a highlight of Metro's calendar (don't worry if you don't speak Arabic; laughter is a universal language). Meanwhile, traditional Arabic music nights are meant to inspire a sense of *saltana*, which means "to be high on music".
Saroulla Center, Hamra Street
+961 (0)1 753 021
metromadina.com

③
Theatre Gemmayze,
Gemmayzeh
Centre stage

As you've no doubt discovered, Beirut's streets are positively packed with cultural centres, galleries and major museums. It should come as no surprise then to learn that the city's artistic clout extends to the stage too.

Set up by famed Lebanese writer, actor and director Joe Kodeih, Theatre Gemmayze opened in 2013 and is part of the city's century-old Collège des Frères du Sacré-Coeur. The 317-seat venue hosts local and international productions, including everything from children's plays to comedy performances, and features a separate hall for exhibitions, conferences and workshops.
Collège du Sacré-Coeur,
Gouraud Street
+961 (0)76 409 109

④
MusicHall, Downtown
Face the music

A night at MusicHall is like a night spent shuffling through your most eclectic playlist – only a little more lively. From US hip-hop to Egyptian folk, this 600-capacity venue features all the musical variety of an international festival.

But it's not just MusicHall's diversity that befits a festival: its stage and sound do too. Founded in 2003 by musical maestro, politician and former judge on the Arabic *X Factor* Michel Elefteriades, the aim was to create an environment in which artists could play well in flawless acoustic conditions. It proved so flawless that in 2013 he created another: MusicHall now has a sister venue on the waterfront.
Starco Center, Omar Daouk Street
+961 (0)1 371 236
themusichall.com

Cinemas
Film first

❶
Metropolis, Ashrafieh
Reel deal

Metropolis opened in 2006; the Israeli-Lebanese war started the very next day. In the midst of such shocking events the cinema became a sort of shelter, with screenings held for the displaced. In the years since its mission has only grown more brave: today the independent cinema visits refugee camps across the region to bring film to the disadvantaged.

Back in the city, however, this non-profit picturehouse is comfortably the best place in Beirut to see foreign and independent film. Metropolis shows subtitled original-language flicks across two screening rooms, each seating about 270. Its programme comprises retrospectives on the likes of Werner Herzog, genre-based film cycles and annual events such as the Beirut International Film Festival.
Sofil Centre, Michel Butros Street
+961 (0)1 204 080
metropoliscinema.net

Beirut on film

01 Hors La Vie, 1991:
Inspired by the kidnapping of French journalist Roger Auque during the Lebanon hostage crisis, this thrilling Maroun Bagdadi-directed picture sees a French photographer abducted and held hostage in war-ravaged Beirut.

02 Beyrouth Fantôme, 1998:
This thriller from director Ghassan Salhab details a conflict between friends, one of whom has seemingly come back from the dead. The narrative is cut with footage of the actors discussing the film, lending it a personal take on the effects of the war.

03 Un Homme Perdu, 2007:
Based on the life and work of French photographer Antoine d'Agata, this film stars Alexander Siddig as a man who goes missing in Beirut – and is determined to stay lost.

04 Je Veux Voir, 2008:
The third feature from Joana Hadjithomas and Khalil Joreige casts Catherine Deneuve opposite the fiercely talented Rabih Mroué. The landscapes are gorgeous and the film captures Lebanon's war-torn complexities.

05 Every Day is a Holiday, 2009: Dima El-Horr's first feature is a genre-busting road film about three feisty women who set out to visit their men in prison.

06 The Insult, 2017:
Featuring top-notch performances from cast and crew alike, Ziad Doueiri's courtroom drama sees a trivial disagreement spiral out of control until it threatens to consume the entire city.

Media round-up
Eyes and ears

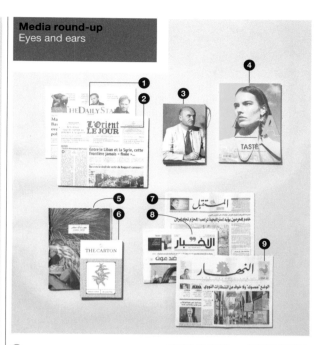

① Media
Read all about it

With such a strong art scene it's no surprise that Beirut's publishing industry is thriving too. ❶ *The Daily Star* is the city's English-language daily, while ❷ *L'Orient Le Jour* is a French-language broadsheet. ❸ *Samandal* contains comics and photographs and, for the above issue, collaborated with the Arab Image Foundation (*see page 95*). Fashion title ❹ *A Magazine* features all the style you'd expect from publisher Aïshti and visual-culture publication ❺ *Journal Safar* is put together by design firm Studio Safar. One of the city's best print titles, ❻ *The Carton* offers readers a savvy snapshot of Middle Eastern food culture. Meanwhile, ❼ *Al Mustaqbal*, ❽ *Al Ahkbar* and ❾ *An Nahar* are three leading Arabic-language dailies.

Radio

01 Radio Liban: This is a refuge for serious music fans with eclectic tastes.
radioliban.gov.lb

02 Sawt Lebnan: The country's first commercial radio station began broadcasting in 1975 and has been going strong since.

03 Vibe Lebanon: Launched from a small back room in the Beirut suburbs in 1998, Vibe was the Middle East's first internet radio station and offers down-tempo techno spiked with jazz and hip-hop.
vibelebanon.com

04 Light FM: From jazz, rock, folk and funk to today's pop hits and yesterday's classics, this is feel-good music at its finest.
radiolightfm.com

Design and architecture
—— Built environment

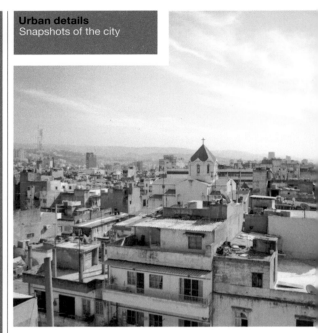

Beirut's skyline has taken a real battering over the past few decades. The 1975 to 1990 civil war not only devastated much of the city but also paved the way for unregulated building and corrupt property deals that continue to produce a swathe of uninspiring luxury tower blocks and malls. The result is a mish-mash of styles that can feel jarring at first glance. But there's more to Beirut than meets the eye.

The Lebanese capital has its own visual rhythm. On top of the beautiful examples of Ottoman-era architecture, it also boasts numerous lesser-known early 20th-century and brutalist buildings, plus some truly soul-lifting reinterpretations of mosques and churches and several world-class contemporary projects. Head out on foot to discover this ancient city's many layers.

①
Old Mercedes taxis, citywide
Familiar face

If you hop in a shared taxi in Beirut (locally known as a *servees*), the chances are it will be an old Mercedes Benz. These wonderful relics from the 1980s have been plying the streets for decades and their drivers have often been around for much longer.

It's not exactly clear why so many Mercs ended up in Lebanon; taxi drivers will tell you that it's because they're the best-built cars around, even if some are so old they have holes in the footwell. Look out for "The Lebanon Taxi", a pimped-out version with the Lebanese flag painted on everything from its bonnet to the headrests.

Did someone say cedar tree?

③
Old lighthouse, Manara
Shining light

A lighthouse has stood in
this spot since the early 19th
century, although this iteration
dates back to 1957. It was
decommissioned during the
15-year civil war and bombed
twice before being brought back
into service in 1993. At roughly
27 metres tall, the tower once
dwarfed the neighbourhood.

It was eventually shut down
in 2003 when an 18-storey
high-rise was built in front
of it and replaced by a newer
lighthouse on the Corniche.
Both are maintained by the
Chebli family, who have looked
after Beirut's lighthouses for
more than 150 years.
Bliss Street

②
Yazan Halwani's murals,
citywide
Grown-up graffiti

The work done by this
Lebanese artist is worlds
away from the scrawls seen
on unlucky train carriages.
Yazan Halwani's murals are
characterised by clouds of
Arabic calligraphy cloaking
portraits of symbolic Lebanese
figures and can be found
decorating walls across town.

At the start of Hamra Street,
the face of iconic Lebanese
performer Sabah watches the
traffic below. On Bliss Street
another mural immortalises Ali
Abdullah, a homeless man who
died one cold winter's night. Yet
another shows a Muslim boy
and a Christian girl from the
classic wartime film *West Beirut*
sharing candyfloss. A fourth
shows eternally popular singer
Fairouz. Political, heartfelt and
visually compelling, Halwani's
pieces have become a treasured
part of the cityscape.

④
Arabic script
Sleight of hand

Arabic calligraphy has evolved enormously over the centuries, taking on new forms to adapt to regional preferences and the growing demand first for written texts and then for printed work. The version you will see on most shop signs in Beirut is *ruqaa*, a simplified version of the more complex *naskh* script developed under the Ottomans for bureaucratic purposes. *Ruqaa* translates as "a piece of cloth", so-called because it was often written on small scraps of paper. Easy to read and to print, it's the closest style to basic Arabic handwriting.

Less common is *nastaliq*, although it's popular for retro Orientalised signs, such as for restaurant Kahwet Leila. It's easy to read and print, and combines *naskh* with *taliq*, the "hanging" script that gives *nastaliq* its characteristic flair.

City shapes
A modernist's paradise

①
Police station, Ashrafieh
Stern face of the law

With its repeating concrete egg-crate façade, this police station has a sternness to it that befits its function. As such, it is a clear example of how brutalism was once used by governments across the world for buildings that needed to exude authority.

Details about the who, the why and the when are scant but local experts suggest it was built in the 1970s by the architect who designed a similar-looking station on Gouraud Street in Gemmayzeh. What we do know is that it was part of a local attempt in the 1960s and early 1970s to use architecture to provide a coherent visual identity for Lebanon's newly created modern institutions, from police stations to post offices.
Ashrafieh Street

②
Ashrafieh brutalism, Sursock and Furn el Hayek
Concrete jungle

As the economy boomed between the 1950s and 1970s, Beirut experienced a wave of urbanisation. Construction engulfed many neighbourhoods and high-density living became the norm, transforming pockets such as Sursock and Furn el Hayek (both in Ashrafieh).

Today this area is peppered with brutalist-style, concrete apartment blocks that were constructed both before the 15-year war – such as Maurice Hindié's 1972 Chammaa Building – and after, including Atelier d'Architectes Associés' 1996 Le Select (*pictured, right*). While the concrete draws on the work of Le Corbusier, the raw-material look was favoured by architects as a trend rather than an ideological practice.

Beirut's Jewish remnants

The only remaining synagogue in Beirut, Maghen Abraham, is never used and unfortunately can't be visited for security reasons. Located in the former Jewish neighbourhood of Wadi Abu Jamil, right by the Grand Serail, it was heavily damaged during the 1975 to 1990 civil war, including by Israeli shelling, and renovations only began in 2009. The spacious two-storey building was built in 1926 at the same time as a nearby Jewish school (demolished in 2003).

The only other evidence of Beirut's Jewish heritage is the overgrown Beth Alamen cemetery on Damascus Road. Dating back to 1829, more than 3,000 people are buried here. Sadly it's not open to the public either.

Judaism was – and is – among the 18 sects explicitly recognised and protected by the constitution and from the early 1900s, Lebanon's Jewish community built educational and religious institutions across the country. Jewish residents have described their community from that time as well-integrated and respected. The population peaked in the 1950s at roughly 10,000 but dwindled due to various wars. These days, the remaining 200 or so Jews live under the radar.

③
Interdesign Showroom,
Clemenceau
Concrete beauty

This extraordinary building seems to almost fragment and rearrange itself as you walk past. The brutalist tower was conceived by Khalil and Georges Khoury to be a shop front for their family's furniture range and work started on the building a few months before the start of the 15-year civil war in the mid-1970s.

The project was paused for two decades because of the war, with the crane remaining on site the whole time, before finally being finished in 1997. Khalil, father of renowned architect Bernard Khoury, was a huge proponent of the modernist movement, as evidenced in his use of *béton brut* (literally "raw concrete") for the bunker-like exterior. The indented sections and angled glass windows shield the cleverly interconnected interior from the strong midday Mediterranean sun while simultaneously maximising natural light.
Rome Street
+961 (0)1 360 300
interdesign.com.lb

④
Koujak-Jaber, Ramlet al-Baida
Windows to the soul

Sometimes referred to as
the gruyère building after the
hole-ridden Swiss cheese, this
residential block's distinctive
round "windows" are unique
in Beirut. In fact, they are not
windows but part of a façade
covering the balconies behind,
forming a kind of screen.

Completed in 1964,
Koujak-Jaber was designed by
Arab-American architect Victor
Bisharat, one of the men behind
California's Disneyland and the
Martyrs' Memorial in Amman,
Jordan. Bisharat's creation
is part of the experimental
approach to façades seen
across Beirut at the time.
Farid Trad Street

In the house

The state-commissioned
1963-built Maison de l'Artisan
was designed by Pierre Neema
and Jacques Aractingi. Located
by the sea in Minet el Hosn, its
structural columns are pointed
arches, part of that period's
shift towards creating a local
architectural identity.
+961 (0)1 368 461

⑤
Gefinor Center, Clemenceau
Office life

This sprawling business and
retail complex comprises a
20-storey tower, three six-
storey buildings and a three-
storey block. In partnership
with local maverick Assem
Salam (*see page 116*), it was
designed by Austrian-born
architect Victor Gruen, who
was regarded as the inventor of
the modern US shopping mall.

Gefinor Center is an
imposing feat of glass and
concrete that carves out several
tree-lined squares from the
busy neighbourhood. The five
blocks were built in the late
1960s, in the heat of Beirut's
love affair with modernist
architecture. It was one of
the first complexes of its size
in the Middle East when it
was completed – and remains
equally impressive today.
Clemenceau Street

⑥
EDL, Mar Mikhael
Electrifying architecture

The state utility company's
lacklustre performance may
be the butt of ongoing jokes –
neatly expressed by the usually
half-lit neon "Electricité du
Liban" sign on the side of their
headquarters – but this is a
serious piece of architecture.
A Lebanese-French collective
called CETA, led by architects
Jacques Aractingi and Pierre
Neema, won a competition to
design the soaring office block,
which was completed in 1972.

Its boxy design draws
inspiration from Brazilian
modernists such as Oscar
Niemeyer, with a park at street
level that was meant to be
open to the public but is now
fenced off. Note the expansive
geometric *claustra* (perforated
wall) added to block direct
sunlight on the southern side.
Armenia Street

Now isn't that a beauty?

Ottoman legacy
Old Beirut

Ottoman-era abodes

Any stroll through Beirut's better preserved neighbourhoods – Gemmayzeh, Ashrafieh, Zokak el Blat and so on – will turn up examples of traditional Lebanese homes from the late 19th century. From the outside they're distinguishable by their solid square shape, triple pointed-arch windows and often a red-tiled roof. Within, the ceilings are high and the space is normally dominated by a large central room that all other rooms open onto, with vaulted archways and arcades, and usually a large balcony. All of it was designed to increase air ventilation and keep the space cool in summer.

The most impressive of these buildings were built for the elite of Lebanon as mansions, palaces and major government buildings. They are not strictly Ottoman in style but rather part of a revival movement blended with Islamic, Italianate and other elements.

Architectural area

Named after the French First World War leader, Clemenceau is home to dozens of spectacular old mansions, including that of veteran Druze leader Walid Jumblatt. The 19th-century Ecole Supérieure des Affaires campus is particularly magnificent.

1

Corm Building, Mathaf
Brave new world

The gleaming white Corm
Building must have been
visible from miles away back in
1928 when it was surrounded
by fields. It was designed not by
an architect but by Lebanese
writer and industrialist Charles
Corm, who was inspired by the
expressionist skyscrapers he
saw on a trip to New York.

That trip won him a
regional Ford Motor Company
dealership and this building was
initially a car-assembly factory.
It later became his family home
and is now being turned into a
cultural foundation. Knock and
ask to see the lovely garden.
Habib Bacha el Saad Street
cormgarden.com

*Admiration
at your
service*

2

Villa Salem, Clemenceau
White lines

With its curving balconies
and *claustra* inserts, this ivory-
coloured building demands
admiration. French architect
Lucien Cavro was influenced
by Le Corbusier when he
designed Villa Salem in the
1930s and this was one of the
first buildings in Beirut to use
the Dom-Ino principles of
the Swiss-French maverick's
prototype for open-plan mass
housing. Its streamlined
volume also references the
Bauhaus movement.

Villa Salem became a
restaurant in the 1990s before
being restored by Nizar Fawwaz
under the auspices of the Arab
Center for Architecture (*see page
113*). Today it houses the Dar
El-Nimer centre (*see page 87*).
America Street
+961 (0)1 367 013
darelnimer.org

③

Clock Tower, Downtown
Telling time

At the centre of historic
Nejmeh Square stands a
1930s clock tower, a present
from Lebanese-Brazilian
émigré Michel Abed to the
government. This landmark
is locally known as the Abed
Clock despite now being
sponsored by Rolex.

Designed by Lebanese-
Armenian architect Mardiros
Altounian, it combines beaux
arts elements (Altounian
studied at Paris's École des
Beaux Arts) and extreme
vertical lines that evoke the
expressionist and futurist
architectural movements. It
was one of the only Downtown
structures to survive the
15-year civil war without any
damage due to the fact it had
previously been moved to
enable excavations below the
square. Altounian also designed
the parliament building
opposite, which is more
traditionally Islamic in style.
Nejmeh Square

④

Opera Building, Downtown
Silver screen

This was just one of many
cinemas (despite its name,
it was never an opera house)
on Beirut's historic Martyrs'
Square, back when it was a
bustling hub rather than a
tiresome extended roundabout.
Now the Opera Building –
and its right-hand neighbour
– are the only two pre-war
buildings that remain.

Designed in the early
1930s by Lebanese architect
Bahjat Abdel Nour, the Opera
Building didn't open its doors
until 1945. Monumental round
pilasters give the building a
neoclassical grandeur common
among Egyptian revival
buildings, mixed with art
deco details. Today it houses
a Virgin Megastore but you
can still admire the sweeping
staircase entrance.
Martyrs' Square

Down by the water

The reclaimed land that
comprises Beirut Waterfront
was built atop the Normandy
wartime landfill and
debris generated by the
reconstruction of Downtown.
Owned by Solidere, the
land is worth about LBP15trn
and hosts bars, clubs
and venues.

Golden age glamour

Lebanon's so-called
golden age during the
1960s and early 1970s
saw the country in the
ascendancy, a playground
for film stars, spies and
royalty. Three buildings
in particular are tied up
with this hallowed period.

01 **Saint-George Hotel,
Ein el Mraysseh:** Built in
1932, this former jet-set
favourite was designed
by a French firm with
Lebanese engineer-
architect Antoine Tabet
and is considered an icon
of modern architecture.
It was gutted during the
1975 to 1990 civil war and
never reopened due to a
legal battle with Solidere,
although its yacht club
sometimes hosts parties
(*see page 123*).
stgeorges-yachtclub.com

02 **Phoenicia Hotel, Ein el
Mraysseh:** Designed in
the 1950s by US architect
Edward Durell Stone, the
Phoenicia opened in 1961
and became an instant hit
with the rich and famous.
The second, taller tower
was added in the 1960s
by local architect Joseph
Philippe Karam. It was
destroyed during the
Battle of the Hotels and
didn't reopen until 2000.
phoeniciabeirut.com

03 **Sporting Club, Manara:**
While today it's a
feast of concrete and
colourful sun shades,
Sporting Club (*see
page 122*) started off
as a beach shack. It
became a popular spot
for businessmen to pop
in for a lunchtime swim
and is still the city's best
sunning spot.
+961 (0)1 742 200

1

The Egg, Downtown
Brutalist bubble

This UFO-like building's curved
exterior has led to it being
nicknamed the Egg, the Dome,
the Bubble and the Soap. It
was once a 1,000-seat cinema,
part of the avant garde Beirut
City Center shopping and
office complex, designed by
local architect Joseph Philippe
Karam in the 1960s but never
finished. Having designed a
raised cinema, he had to give
it a shape and plumped for
an oval.

Located on a former
frontline, the Egg endured
years of heavy conflict.
From the late 1990s it was a
nightclub and cultural space
until Solidere sold the land in
2005. Plans to incorporate it
into a hotel have stalled, leaving
its shell lying in limbo.
*Opposite Markazieh Building,
Bechara el Khoury Street*

②
Holiday Inn, Ein el Mraysseh
Seaside snipers' nest

Designed by André Wogenscky, a student of Le Corbusier, along with Lebanese architect Maurice Hindieh, this brutalist building opened in 1975 to great fanfare. It boasted a pool overlooking the Mediterranean and a rotating rooftop restaurant, the husk of which is still visible.

Within months, however, it became a key site in the 15-year civil war, which caused extensive damage to the concrete exterior and left the interior covered in militia graffiti. Its future is uncertain, with a highly charged debate over whether it should be pulled down to make space for something new or renovated as is. In the meantime, it's an army base where tanks are parked.
Fakhreddine/Omar Daouk Street

Beit Beirut, Sodeco
Museum of memories

Originally a set of apartments called Beit Barakat, after the wealthy Barakat family who owned it, this neo-Ottoman building was bought by the Beirut municipality in 2003 for a one-of-a-kind memory museum and cultural space (*see page 88*). The bottom two floors were built in the 1920s by Youssef Aftimus, who also designed Beirut's Moorish-style city hall, with the top two floors added a decade later.

Located on a key frontline intersection, Beit Beirut later became a snipers' hideout. Renovation architect Youssef Haidar controversially chose to leave its war scars untouched, repairing only where necessary and using bare metal to make his interventions obvious.
Sodeco Square
beitbeirut.org

④
Murr Tower, Downtown
Long shadow

Composed of 40 floors of grey concrete that jut into the sky, the Murr Tower is a Beirut landmark. Under construction as the civil war began in 1975, it was intended to be Lebanon's World Trade Center. Instead, as with the Holiday Inn (*see left*), it became a vantage point for militias, with the basement rumoured to have been used as a prison.

Today it's heavily associated with death and its owner, Solidere, is unsure about what to do with it. For now it's used as a military post so don't get too close while taking pictures.
Fakhreddine/General Fouad Chehab Street

Past and present

Founded in 2008, the Arab Center for Architecture aims to raise awareness about the region's modern architectural heritage and how to protect it. Run by George Arbid, it boasts a valuable archive of regional architects and buildings.
arab-architecture.org

Monument men

01 Rafik Hariri, Ein el Mraysseh and Downtown: There are two statues of Lebanon's former prime minister, who continues to tower over Lebanese politics. One, opposite the Phoenicia Hotel, marks the place where he was killed when his motorcade blew up in 2005. The other is by the Grand Serail.

02 Riad al-Solh, Downtown: The first prime minister of independent Lebanon helped implement the National Pact, which is the sectarian power division system that still exists today. His Riad al-Solh Square statue sports the traditional Ottoman *tarboosh* hat.

03 Martyrs' Statue, Downtown: This commemorates the hanging of Lebanese nationalists by the Ottomans in 1916. The heavy damage that the statue sustained during the 15-year civil war is still visible – a purposeful decision by the restorers.

04 Khalil Gibran, Downtown: Watching over the peaceful Gibran Khalil Gibran Garden is a bust of the famous Lebanese writer and artist. His best-known work *The Prophet* has been translated into dozens of languages.

05 Samir Kassir, Downtown: This statue immortalises an academic and journalist who was assassinated in 2005. Located by the *An-Nahar* paper where he worked, it overlooks the Aga Khan Award-winning Samir Kassir Square.

Religious buildings
Mosques and churches

1

Mohammad al-Amin Mosque,
Downtown
Power play

A hugely political piece of
architecture, this golden
temple of Saudi stone was
a controversial addition to
Martyrs' Square due to its
ostentatious size and style.
Designed by local architect
Azmi Fakhouri, it was the pet
project of assassinated former
prime minister Rafik Hariri,
who even selected the shade of
blue for the ceramic domes.
   Plans date back decades
but work only began in
2003. The exterior comprises
two interlocking volumes,
one defined by the street
grid and another facing
Mecca, and recalls Istanbul's
Byzantine-era Hagia
Sophia or Cairo's Ottoman
Muhammad Ali Mosque.
The lavish interior features
intricate Islamic calligraphy,
Turkish tiles, Persian carpets
and a six-tonne chandelier.
Martyrs' Square

② Saint Anthony the Great
Church, Monot
In the round

The unusual circular exterior
of this Maronite church
features rustic Lebanese
masonry around the sides,
paired with vertically placed
cut stone around the façade
and a lid-like rooftop, making
it a curious mix of styles. Little
is known about the architect
but it was probably built in
the 1960s.
   A wonderfully modern
re-interpretation of traditional
Christian architecture, the
roundness of the building
connotes a dome, despite
its absence. The interior is
strikingly simple – white
walls and very few religious
paintings – and offset by
beautiful woodwork that
lines the entire room.
Furn el Hayek Street

❸ Khashoggi Mosque,
Horsh Beirut
Concrete worship

Located opposite what remains
of Beirut's ancient forest
(*see page 123*), Khashoggi
Mosque is a fascinating mix
of modernist instincts infused
with traditional elements.
Renowned local architect and
heritage activist Assem Salam
designed the contemporary
mosque in the late 1960s.
This was after he finished
both the Pan Am building
and Tourism Ministry and
was searching for a more
local architectural identity.
   The arabesque geometry of
the concrete roof atop the main
building replaces the traditional
dome and is echoed inside.
Note the pointed archways in
the outdoor courtyard, which
were designed perpendicular
to the street in order to initially
hide their true form, only
revealing themselves as you
enter the space.
November 22 Street

Contemporary
New kids on the block

① USJ's Campus for Innovation
and Sport, Mathaf
Inspiring study centre

Defined by voids, cut-aways
and indents, the ambitious
Saint Joseph University
complex comprises six
unevenly shaped structures
set apart and linked by mid-
air bridges and walkways.

Local firms 109 Architectes
and Youssef Tohmé created
various concrete façades,
including thick walls punctured
with small, deep-set windows
and geometric *claustra* skins
inspired by the Arabic version
of an oriel window known as a
mashrabiya. This blend of the
austere and the playful, the
solid and the porous, comes
together beautifully under
the Mediterranean sun, with
shadow and light dancing in
and out of the buildings.
Damascus Street
+961 (0)1 421 000
usj.edu.lb

American University of Beirut's Issam Fares Institute, Ein el Mraysseh
Another planet

Surrounded by red-roofed Ottoman-era buildings and grassy squares, Zaha Hadid Architects' university department building is unapologetic in its other-worldliness – and it won an Aga Khan Award as a result. The late Iraqi-British architect studied maths at AUB so it's fitting that this mind-bending form found a home here.

Entering along the building's narrow walkway feels a lot like boarding a spaceship and the dynamic structure includes a 21-metre-long cantilevered section that looms over the gnarled trees below. The fair-faced concrete exterior features slanted windows echoed in relief patterns across the walls, while the interior's intersecting circulation routes are designed to foster interaction and dialogue.
Bliss Street
+961 (0)1 340 460
aub.edu.lb/ifi

③
Beirut Terraces, Downtown
Sunset views

❹
East Village, Mar Mikhael
Lego life

In a city lacking public space, your terrace can be your world, something that Swiss firm Herzog & de Meuron understands well. Made of different sized floors arranged in various combinations, Beirut Terraces' staggered apartments enjoy views over city and sea.

Perforated overhangs provide shade, as well as floor plates thick enough to retain the heat of the day and release it during the night. Coming in at 119 metres, the jagged silhouette of this brilliant white high-rise cuts an imposing figure, setting it apart from the bland towers of glass rising around it.
Ahmad Shawki Street
beirutterraces.com

This stack of irregularly shaped blocks of rusting brown, deep red and granite grey is an unconventional residential building that grew out of a commission from gallerist Naila Kettaneh-Kunigk, whose Galerie Tanit *(see page 92)* occupies the ground floor.

Local architect Jean-Marc Bonfils added 10 two-storey flats, with soaring ceilings that echo those of traditional Lebanese houses, as well as a pair of penthouses and a simplex. Mixing traditional wood and stone with metal, the structure features cantilevered sections that protrude and extend in surprising places.
Armenia Street
jmbonfils.com/projects

Sport and fitness
──── Take the plunge

For Beirutis, self-image doesn't stop at luxury handbags and souped-up cars; it includes a taut and tanned set of buns and a rippling panel of abs. But where to work out in this built-up metropolis stifled by traffic and lacking in large public spaces?

To help combat this conundrum, we've eschewed our regular format of tailored runs and mapped-out cycle routes in favour of spotlighting our favourite outdoor destinations. Think leathery sunseekers fishing on the Corniche and runners in the latest garb looping the growing greenery of Horsh Beirut. It's in these spots that you'll be able to clock some kilometres whether on two wheels or on foot, all the while soaking up that vibrant outdoors lifestyle.

In case the weather wavers while you're in town, we've also listed a multifunctional gym space with climbing walls to boot and a lofty yoga studio that's more sweat and tears than casual stretching. Finally, to ensure that you're spruced for a Beiruti night on the tiles we've pointed you towards some top grooming spots.

The great outdoors
Dive in

①
Corniche, Manara
Sea air

From May to October, days in Beirut become long, torturous and sweaty. Only once the working day ends (or before it kicks off for the early birds) can its residents escape the stifling heat of the car-clogged streets and head to the city's cooling stretches of Mediterranean coastline.

For most this means the Corniche, where the endless tower blocks and snarling traffic give way to a seaside esplanade: several kilometres long and wide enough to accommodate a cycle lane, benches, palm trees and plenty of pedestrians. At certain spots there are also makeshift squash and tennis courts, diving platforms from craggy rocks and plenty of perches from which to fish. As night begins to fall, the well-dressed joggers, dripping cyclists and groups of gung ho divers are joined by musicians, couples walking hand in hand and revellers.

2

Sporting Club, Manara
Glam rock

Beirut is a city of beach-goers
and sun-worshippers – so
much so that Lebanon's golden
era in the 1960s revolved
around its coastal restaurants
and clubs. Even during the
1975 to 1990 civil war,
residents would take advantage
of lulls in the fighting to swim
in the sea and sunbathe.

One of the oldest and
best-known spots is Sporting
Club, a family-run joint
founded in 1953. It's morphed
from a shack on the rocks
to a vast concrete institution
complete with three pools,
a squash court, kayak and
stand-up paddle-board
hire, sunbathing platforms,
Pigeon's Rock views, and a
restaurant and café that both
serve great seafood.
Corniche, Manara
+961 (0)1 742 200

③

Saint-George Yacht Club and
Marina, Ein el Mraysseh
Welcome to the club

The abandoned shell of
Saint-George Hotel (*see page
111*), which was razed by the
car bomb that killed then prime
minister Rafik Hariri in 2005,
is now home to a cracking
beach club. Its three larger
pools and one children's pool
(open daily) sit in the shadow
of the fabled hotel, with vistas
onto the Mediterranean.
There's a poolside bar and
restaurant that stay open late
into the evening and host some
of the best parties in town.
Rafik el Hariri Avenue
+691 3 958 379
stgeorges-yachtclub.com

Walk this way

Ecotourism company Liban
Trek offers day and multi-
day walks. Hike through the
Qadisha valley to see early
Christian monasteries tucked
into the cliffside or visit the
Danniyeh district for trails
along wooded gorges and
dramatic cliffs.
libantrek.com

④

Horsh Beirut
Tree huggers

The congested capital's
historic pine forest has had
a rocky history. It was
deforested by the Crusaders,
Mamluks and Ottomans
and cleared to make way
for a casino in 1917, then
a horse-racing track in 1921
(which still stands). Most
recently it has been a victim of
a government blockade for two
decades following the 15-year
civil war in an effort to deter
political gatherings and protests.

But after years of
campaigning by local groups,
the 30-hectare sliver that
still remains of the original
forest reopened to the public
in 2016. It's now one of the
only green lungs within city
limits and its grounds offer an
uninterrupted expanse of paths
to run, cycle and walk along.

①

Athletes Anonymous,
Mar Mikhael
Pull your weight

This tidy workout spot is
located next to Tawlet (*see page
27*) – a handy place for a post-
workout lunch – and tucks
plenty of activities into a
surprisingly compact space.
There's an organic juice bar, an
outdoor calisthenics terrace and
a small but well-stocked studio
upstairs for private sessions.

On your way downstairs
you'll pass the six-metre
climbing wall and enter the
main gym, with weightlifting,
cardio and boxing areas that
are connected by a running
track. Off to the side is a larger
studio where TRX suspension,
Pilates and yoga take place.
Non-members can pay by
class or opt for a day pass.
Armenia Street
+961 (0)1 560 507
athletesanonymous.com

2

Yoga Souk, Saifi Village
Bend the rules

Located in a restored building
in Saifi Village, complete
with soaring vaulted ceilings,
this studio specialises in
dynamic Vinyasa yoga. The
morning Ashtanga class runs
continuously from 06.15 until
10.00 every weekday. As new
students arrive, the teacher
runs them through the
sequence of movements, which
each individual can then
practise for as little or as long
as they please.

"It's like a private class but
with 20 people around you,"
says co-founder Sarah Trad.
Also on the roster are beginner
lessons, classes matched to
music and sessions for kids.
Don't say we didn't warn you:
it's a sweaty, physical affair.
752 Said Akl Street
+961 (0)81 608 607
yogasouk.com

Grooming
Look sharp

1

Private by N, Saifi Village
One to one

Those seeking a more low-
key affair than the glam salons
in abundance around the city
should head to Private by N.
Co-founder Nizar Boushilian
is the sole hairdresser, offering
both men's and women's cuts
and styling. "It's only one chair,
it's only by appointment and
it's only one client. He or she
gets the best attention," says
Boushilian. The single chair
is tucked inside a Saifi Village-
based concept store, the
colourful floor tiles of which
were salvaged from a former
Lebanese house.
Said Akl Street
+961 3 589 070
saifivillage.com

2

Phil & Joe, Gemmayzeh
Memory lane

While playing poker one night,
friends and well-travelled
businessmen Joseph Aoun and
Philippe Skaff lamented the
lack of an upmarket barbershop
in Lebanon. From that
conversation Phil & Joe was
born, opening its first location
in Gemmayzeh in 2016.

"The intention was to
recreate the atmosphere of the
old Italian-American vintage
barbershop," says Skaff.
"It's mixed with an industrial
look and the feel of a high-
end boutique," he adds. The
wooden counter and leather
chairs are tinged with nostalgia
– as is the service, which
includes hot towels before
and after a shave, as well as
a head and neck massage.
Gouraud Street
+961 (0)1 443 051
philandjoebarbers.com

Keep the peace
——
The rush
of the city
stops here

L'Espace Al Bustan, Beit Mery
Tonic water

This tranquil spot requires a 15km drive up the hill to Beit Mery, where the views from Al Bustan Hotel's (*see page 20*) lofty perch and the cool, pine-scented air provide some reprieve from the hazy city below. A separate building from the mid-century hotel, this traditional Ottoman house dates back two centuries and was painstakingly restored and transformed into a spa. The original stone façade remains and colourful Tunisian tiles have been added.

L'Espace Al Bustan features a workout room, yoga studio, steam room, sauna, hammam, indoor pool and ice pool – but the real draw is the menu of relaxing, restorative treatments.
Al Bustan Hotel
+961 (0)3 752 003
hotelalbustan.com

Catch you on the flip side!

Walks
—— Take to
the streets

Getting around Beirut
is best done on foot.
Sure, you may have
to dodge cavernous
potholes, navigate military
checkpoints and brave the
traffic when the pavement
disappears altogether
but walking allows you
to take in the city and
all its quirks at a more
digestible pace. It makes
it much easier to duck into
peculiar boutiques, peer
past fences into grand
palaces and weave your
way through narrow side
streets. We've mapped out
four urban trails to help
you find your stride.

Downtown/
Ashrafieh
Layers of history

First settled more than 4,000
years ago, making it one of the
oldest continuously inhabited
cities in the world, Beirut has
a long and fascinating history.
Excavations following the
destruction of Downtown
during the 1975 to 1990 civil
war unearthed layers of
Phoenician, Hellenistic, Roman,
Byzantine, Arab, Crusader and
Ottoman remains – although
sadly only a few sites have been
preserved for the public to enjoy.

This walk takes in ancient
and modern layers of Lebanon,
with Downtown home to many
physical reminders of its darker
days, and finishes with a spot
of shopping and drinking in
some of the most beautiful
parts of Ashrafieh.

Ancient and modern
Downtown walk

Begin with a drip coffee
and homemade granola at
❶ *Backburner* in postcard-
pretty Saifi Village. This area
was carefully reconstructed
after the war as an upscale arts
quarter, populated by designers
such as Bokja.

Head to the southwest corner
of Martyrs' Square and enter
the ❷ *Mohammad al-Amin
Mosque* – women should take
the abaya cloak provided.
With its domes and minarets,
this Ottoman-style building
(*see page 109*) is a recent (and
controversial) addition to the
square; it's known locally as
the Rafik Hariri Mosque after
its patron, the divisive prime
minister who was assassinated
(allegedly by Hezbollah) in
2005. This precipitated the
end of the Syrian occupation
and is key to understanding
Lebanon's polarised political

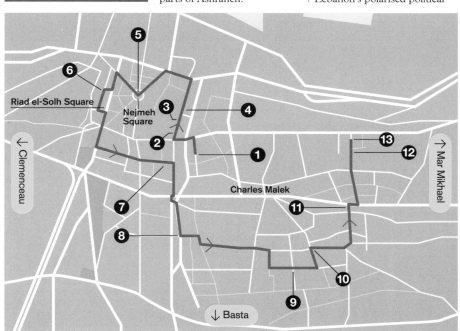

landscape. Adjacent to the mosque, ❸ *Rafik Hariri's tomb* shows how large his memory looms, be it reviled or revered.

Exit left from the mosque and pass the bullet-riddled ❹ *Martyrs' Statue*, a monument to those who died resisting the Ottoman occupation. Turn left, then pass through the first army post and into historic ❺ *Nejmeh Square*, home to the city's parliament. Once the beating heart of Beirut, this patch is now a ghost town thanks to high rent and regional tensions but there's still plenty to see. Don't miss the Saint George Greek Orthodox Cathedral as well as the small archaeological museum (*see page 87*) to its left; to the right is a panoramic view of some neglected ancient ruins.

With parliament on your left, leave the square and head straight to the better-preserved ❻ *Roman baths* at the foot of the Grand Serail, the seat of the government. Veer left into Riad al-Solh Square (named after independent Lebanon's first prime minister) and through the car park behind it. This was once a bustling neighbourhood but Solidere, the company that rebuilt central Beirut after the war, razed it to be redeveloped. A little further on is the surreal war relic known as ❼ *The Egg* (*see page 112*), a former cinema.

Head under the highway and keep left; you're now on Damascus Road, the wartime frontline between east and

west Beirut. It was known as the Green Line, apparently because of how overgrown it became, and many buildings still bear scars. Grab a falafel wrap from either of the almost identical ❽ *Falafel M Sahyoun* shops, run by two estranged brothers who both wanted to carry on their father's business.

Crossing the road, duck into a side street leading to Monot. Turn left at Artist restaurant and stroll past more bullet-pocked buildings into Furn el Hayek, a charming traditional Christian neighbourhood. Cross Lebanon Street, turn right, then left and admire the gleaming white ❾ *Abdallah Bustros Palace*, an Ottoman mansion now home to Liza restaurant (*see page 24*).

Order a glass of something in nearby Bread Republic's ❿ *Wine Room* and, once revived, head right and then left down a street of rundown but beautiful buildings. Just before the main road, pop into ⓫ *6:05* (*see page 57*), a fun place for clothes and accessories.

Cross Charles Malek Avenue, walking north to reach ⓬ *Saint Nicholas Stairs*, the most enchanting of east Beirut's various stairways. Finish on the balcony of the ⓭ *The Grand Meshmosh Hotel*, with some nibbles and a cold drink.

Address book

01 **Backburner**
    Ariss and Kanafani Street
    +961 (0)1 989 343
    thebackburner.com
02 **Mohammad
    al-Amin Mosque**
    Martyrs' Square
03 **Rafik Hariri's tomb**
    Martyrs' Square
04 **Martyrs' Statue**
    Martyrs' Square
05 **Nejmeh Square**
06 **Roman baths**
    Between Banks and
    Capuchins streets
07 **The Egg**
    Bechara el-Khoury Street
08 **Falafel M Sahyoun**
    Damascus Road
    +961 (0)1 659 139
09 **Abdallah Bustros Palace**
    Doumani Street
10 **Wine Room**
    Furn el Hayek Street
    +961 (0)1 201 520
11 **6:05**
    Zen Building,
    Charles Malek Avenue
    +961 (0)1 335 450
    605.com.lb
12 **Saint Nicholas Stairs**
    Between Gouraud and
    Sursock streets
13 **The Grand
    Meshmosh Hotel**
    Saint Nicholas Stairs
    +961 (0)1 563 465
    thegrandmeshmosh.com

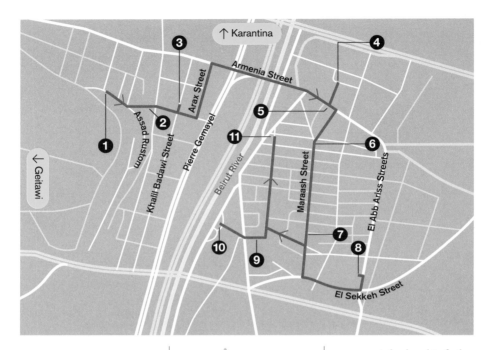

Mar Mikhael/ Bourj Hammoud
Armenian enclave

The main road in Mar Mikhael, Armenia Street, is where the Armenian part of Beirut begins. Most of the community arrived after the genocide of 1915 to 1916 and settled primarily in Bourj Hammoud and the Bekaa Valley town of Anjar.

Since arriving, the Armenians have become renowned for their craftsmanship, particularly jewellery-making. Although slightly run down, this part of town has a wonderful raw energy and provides a fascinating glimpse of another side of Beirut.

Little Armenia
Mar Mikhael/Bourj Hammoud walk

Start by heading to ❶ *Riwaq*, a small café on a peaceful backstreet, where you can have a coffee and a traditional Lebanese breakfast of labneh (creamy strained yoghurt), fresh vegetables and bread. When you're done, walk a few minutes east on Assad Rustom Street and then head left down

an apparent dead-end to find the neglected remains of the ❷ *Old Lebanese coastal railway line*. It once ran from Haifa to Tripoli but was heavily damaged during the war and hasn't been used since.

Continue straight until you reach Khalil Badawi Street, where you'll spot a pink building on the opposite side of the road. Climb to the first floor and you'll find ❸ *Depot-Vente*, a quirky one-stop shop for vintage dresses, old Levi's and retro sunglasses. Browse a while then bear left out the building, then left and left again onto Arax. This road is home to the headquarters of one of the oldest Armenian political parties and features plenty of anti-Turkey graffiti, a common sight around here.

At Armenia Street, turn right and pick your way across the heaving Pierre Gemayel highway. Walk over the pitiful Beirut River, from which an

animal charity once famously rescued an abandoned crocodile, and enter Bourj Hammoud, otherwise known as Lebanon's Little Armenia.

If you're hungry, take the second left after the bridge and grab a spicy Armenian-style wrap from ❹ *Apo* – the Orfali sandwich with barbecued meat and vegetables is hard to beat. If you'd prefer something freshly squeezed, you'll find it at ❺ *Eco Juice* on the right-hand side of the main road. Note the number of jewellery shops around here; it's a trade for which the Armenians have built up a global reputation.

Take the first right after Eco Juice and continue straight onto ❻ *Maraash Street*, a typically lively shopping strip punctuated by Armenian flags, tangles of electrical wires and small Christian shrines. This is a great place to buy Middle Eastern spices and sweets and to admire the outrageous bling of the clothes for sale.

On the left towards the end of the street, watch out for ❼ *Darsko Records*, a tiny vinyl shop run by cratedigger and DJ Ernesto Chahoud. It specialises in funk, soul and disco but opening times are erratic so it's best to call ahead.

When you reach the end of the road, hang a left on El Sekkeh Street and check out the Catholic ❽ *Saint Savior Church*, a wonderful example of Armenian religious architecture. Retrace your steps back to Maraash Street and turn left down the side street with the Abou Naian lingerie shop on the corner. Turn left at the end and you'll soon arrive at an enormous wall covered in colourful ❾ *Yervant Hawarian murals*; the local cinema poster artist's stamp-style images depict famous Lebanese places. Be sure to look up: the extraordinary brutalist windows are part of an abandoned cotton factory complex.

On a grassy knoll in the middle of the nearby main road stands the ❿ *Armenian Genocide Memorial*, one of a number in Lebanon, showing several ghostly figures emerging from their stone plinths. Back at the murals wall, walk straight down the street directly opposite until you reach ⓫ *Badguèr*, a pretty Armenian cultural centre with a cracking restaurant.

Put your feet up and get stuck into some local specialities such as *basterma* (cured beef), *soujouk* (spicy beef sausages), *souboureg* (cheesy pastries) and stuffed vegetables. Badguèr promotes local arts and crafts and is also a great place to ask any questions you have about Armenians in Lebanon.

Address book

01 Riwaq
Assad Rustom Street
+961 81 715 656
02 Old Lebanese coastal railway line
Between Assad Rustom and Bani Kahtan streets
03 Depot-Vente
Khalil Badawi Street
+961 (0)3 200 620
04 Apo
Tiro Street
+961 (0)1 261 789
05 Eco Juice
Armenia Street
+961 (0)1 261 231
06 Maraash Street
07 Darsko Records
Maraash Street
+961 70 990 198
08 Saint Savior Church
Between El Sekkeh and El Abb Ariss streets
09 Yervant Hawarian murals
10 Armenian Genocide Memorial
Sin el-Fil Street
11 Badguèr
Der Melkonian Street
+961 (0)1 240 214
badguer.org

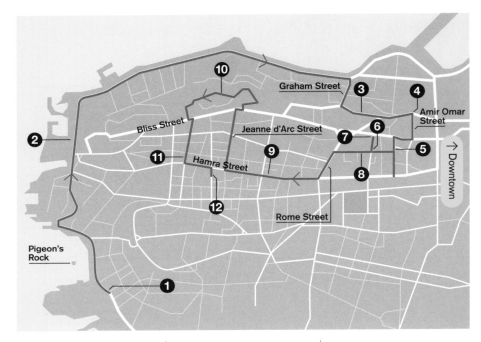

Ras Beirut

Neighbourhood of contradictions

Ras Beirut – encompassing Raoucheh, Clemenceau and, at its heart, Hamra – was Beirut's cosmopolitan and commercial centre until the devastation of the 1975 to 1990 civil war and the subsequent degeneration.

Today, Ras Beirut is a mélange of luxury real-estate developments and crumbling heritage houses, rapid gentrification and small family businesses that have survived for generations, and ongoing urbanisation and backstreets fragranced by orange blossom. This walk will introduce you to this diverse section of the city and help you discover its rich history, witness its wild contradictions and appreciate its beauty and vitality.

Art and architecture
Ras Beirut walk

Start your walk in Raoucheh with a *knafeh bi jibneh* (a syrup-soaked cheesy pastry) from **1** *Ahmad Aouni Hallab & Sons* – this was the first branch of the iconic sweet shop to open outside of Tripoli. Cross the street to take in the stunning cliff known as Pigeon's Rock – and look out for the young men who prove their bravado by diving from it.

Follow the sea north to the **2** *Corniche*, Beirut's most cherished and diverse public space. Here, chit-chatting high-society ladies power-walk past the old fishermen who line the coast from as early as 05.00. Stop in front of Le Bain Militaire and admire the views of the Manara, the old lighthouse, and La Maison Rose, the old pink mansion.

Continue for approximately 20 minutes along the Corniche

until you reach Ain El Mreisseh Mosque. Turn up Graham Street to John Kennedy Street, bearing left onto **3** *Omar Daouk Street*. Here you can wander past some of Beirut's best-preserved Ottoman and French-style houses, including the 19th-century Ladki House with its sandstone walls and the lovely Said Jumblatt House with its gardenia trees.

While on Omar Daouk, pop into **4** *Orient 499* for artisanal

regional crafts (*see page 49*). Opposite is the towering and bullet-ridden Holiday Inn (*see page 49*).

Walk up the incline of Amir Omar Street, then turn right on Clemenceau and left to walk along ⑤ *May Ziadeh Street*. This is one of the few remaining heritage clusters in Ras Beirut. Take in the French mandate structures and the art deco building locally known as Villa Kettaneh. Apparently the four-storey, free-standing wall around it was built to prevent nosy neighbours from peering into the garden.

After touring May Ziadeh, take the perpendicular Jebran Khalil Jebran Street to visit Villa Salem (*see page 110*), a charming 1930s Le Corbusier Dom-Ino-style building in the heart of Beirut. It's now home to ⑥ *Dar El-Nimer* (*see page 87*), which regularly exhibits modern and contemporary cultural productions from Lebanon, Palestine and the wider region.

For a touch more culture, turn right at the corner and you'll find ⑦ *Saleh Barakat Gallery* (*see page 92*). This is an adapted reuse of a historical theatre, Masrah al Madina, and before that (as early as 1969), Cinema Clemenceau (one of the first in the Middle East to show experimental films and cinema of the Soviet Union). Today the modern art gallery is dedicated to showcasing

up-and-coming Lebanese and Arab artists.

Return to the corner and continue west to reach the recently renovated ⑧ *Beyt Amir*. Enjoy a lemonade in the lush garden of this hidden traditional house, which also boasts a changing arts programme.

Head west again, then left on Rome Street and right to walk along Hamra Street. The arrival of establishments such as the Metro Al Madina (*see page 97*) theatre is a nod to the street's pre-war glory and affirmation of Hamra's lasting intellectual and commercial value. Grab a table at ⑨ *Mezyan*, a casual restaurant evoking the lively Hamra of the 1960s. Try the *manti* (Armenian dumplings).

While lunch settles, deviate north along Jeanne d'Arc Street then left on Bliss Street to enter the picturesque upper campus of the ⑩ *American University of Beirut*. Anyone can enter, just leave your ID at reception.

After exploring the campus, meander south down Mahatma Gandhi Street until you reach Hamra again. A left off Hamra takes you to ⑪ *Ferdinand* (*see page 46*) a favourite for a cocktail or beer. Or, if you'd prefer something caffeinated, go two blocks up Hamra and take a right to relax with a *rakweh* (Turkish coffee pot) at the open-air ⑫ *Café Younes*, a coffee shop that's been roasting and brewing since 1935.

Address book

01 Ahmad Aouni
    Hallab & Sons
    General de Gaulle Street
    +961 (0)1 789 999
    hallab.com.lb
02 Corniche
    General de Gaulle Street
03 Omar Daouk Street
    Clemenceau
04 Orient 499
    499 Omar Daouk Street
    +961 (0)1 369 499
    orient499.com
05 May Ziadeh Street
    Clemenceau
06 Dar El-Nimer
    America Street
    +961 (0)1 367 013
    darelnimer.org
07 Saleh Barakat Gallery
    Minkara Building,
    Justinian Street
    +961 (0)1 365 615
    agialart.com
08 Beyt Amir
    America Street
    +961 (0)1 444 110
09 Mezyan
    Rasamny Building,
    Hamra Street
    +961 71 293 015
10 American University
    of Beirut
    Bliss Street
    +961 (0)1 350 000
    aub.edu.lb
11 Ferdinand
    Mahatma Gandhi Street
    +961 (0)1 355 955
12 Café Younes
    Neemat Yafet Street
    +961 (0)1 750 975
    cafeyounes.com

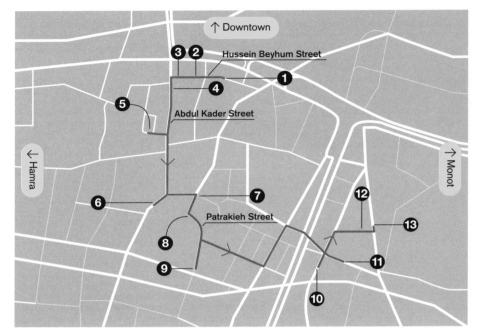

Zokak el Blat
Faded glories

Rapid population growth during the Ottoman rule in the 19th century saw the wealthy build ornate mansions with sprawling orchards in the hills surrounding the city. In 1995, the historic Zokak el Blat quarter (now encompassing Patrakieh and Basta) had 94 heritage buildings but in the decades since the number has dwindled through demolition and reassessment. Many of the mansions now lie in ruins.

This route will take you past a selection of these once glorious buildings and into the hub of antiques dealers in Basta. But we must warn you, food along this route is limited so it's best to tackle this walk over the course of a morning, with the afternoon dedicated to feasting elsewhere in the city.

Grand locations
Zokak el Blat walk

Start the tour on Hussein Beyhum Street, with the mid-19th-century Ottoman-style building that houses the German ❶ *Orient-Institut Beirut.* This mansion, named Villa Maud Farjallah after the leading political activist who lived here, hosted countless social events and formative independence meetings during the 20th century. Head west, past the first side street, and you'll find the ❷ *Ichkhanian Bakery* (closed on Mondays). This Armenian family business has served *lahmadjun* (flat bread topped with spiced mince meat) and a tomatoey vegetarian version since 1946. It's the only food stop on the walk so best to take a beat and savour the freshly baked goods.

Continue west to the last building on the right: ❸ *Heneine Palace.* Built in the

late 1800s, near the end of Ottoman rule, the Moorish-inspired interiors differentiate the grand abode from other palaces of the era. The building fell into ruin after the death of its last owner in 1970 and, despite receiving landmark status in 2010, demolition by

developers looms large. Turn left onto Abdul Kader Street and at the end of the first block is another Ottoman-era mansion overrun by greenery. ❹ *Ziade Palace* on the left was built in 1860 and housed two aristocratic families, the second of which, the Ziades, fled during the civil war.

Pass the Modern University for Business and Science buildings, turn right down the side street and enter the pale-blue wrought-iron gates to visit ❺ *Ashghalouna*. The Friends' Committee of Social Welfare Institutions Islamic Orphanage run this charitable handicraft shop that also serves homestyle Lebanese dishes on Fridays. Return to Abdul Kader Street and continue heading south up the hill. At the top of the incline there's a break in the wall; peer through to see the 1909 French-built sandstone schoolhouse ❻ *Lycée Abdel Kader*, with its thick wooden beams and green shutters.

Cross the street and retrace your steps slightly to nip down past a small carpark towards the quaint and feline-filled grounds of ❼ *Notre Dame de l'Annonciation*, built between 1843 and 1845. Round the corner, heading south past the vine-covered ❽ *Greek Catholic Patriarchate school* that opened in 1925. Continue around the bend and just before the main road, towering on the right is ❾ *Bechara El Khoury*

Palace, another faded and crumbling 19th-century mansion that was home to the first post-independence Lebanese president.

Double back towards the Patriarchate and take the first right, walking downhill. Pass a fruit market and tattoo parlour then take the third left, before walking north and taking the second right through the tunnel (watch your head) that bypasses the main road above. This will deliver you to the heart of the antiques district. Turn right at the crumbling rosy apartment block and start the treasure hunt in the higgledy-piggledy jumble of stalls at the ❿ *Basta souks*.

For a more refined selection of Islamic and Oriental antiques, visit ⓫ *Diwan Ammar* (*see page 54*) by exiting the souks and crossing the road east past the rosy block – now on your right. Next, head back past the same block, turning right and then right again to reach ⓬ *Hamadani Brothers*, the shop run by the nephews of Diwan Ammar owner Youssef Ammar. There are two shopfronts belonging to the brothers, who took over their father's business and now specialise in restoring mid-century furniture. Finish up on the corner at ⓭ *Old Story*, with its furniture from the 1950s to 1970s and a basket full of black-and-white photos: a peek into the country's past.

Out of town
—— Escapes

As easy as it may be to spend your entire stay wiggling your way around the multifarious capital, it would be a shame to miss out on some of the easily reached locations lying a little further afield. Here are a few recommendations to inspire a trip out of town, from pulling up a lounger at one of the beach clubs lining the azure waters of the Batroun coastline to exploring the mountainous landscapes supporting small villages and a burgeoning wine scene. Your cultural and culinary tour of Lebanon continues beyond Beirut's borders.

01

02   03

04

05

06 07

08

Head to:

Baalbeck
This is one of the world's most important archaeological sites, with a vast Roman acropolis. It's also home to the Baalbeck International Festival.

Batroun
Located 53km north of Beirut, Batroun is home to an ancient Phoenician sea wall and several kilometres of limestone coastline dotted with beach clubs and guesthouses.

Bekaa Valley
The strip of land between Mount Lebanon and the Anti-Lebanon Mountains hosts more than a dozen wineries, including Chateau Ksara and Massaya.

Byblos
Just 37km north of Beirut, Byblos is heralded for its World Heritage-listed medieval town and a history that stretches back some 8,000 years.

Chouf District
The mountainous Chouf District is 41km west of Beirut. Come here to hike and explore the arak distilleries and the quaint villages.

01 Beit al Batroun guesthouse
02 Batroun's calm waters are ideal for paddle-boarding
03 Shingle beach of Batroun
04 Jammal restaurant
05–07 Pierre and Friends beach club and its revellers
08 Fruit and vegetables at the food market in Batroun

01

02

03   04

05

06 07

08

Address book

Beit al Batroun, Thoum
Colette Kahil and her French bulldog Kloe are the perfect hosts at this B&B.
beitalbatroun.com

Beit Douma, Douma
Retreat run by owner of Tawlet (*see page 27*) Kamal Mouzawak and fashion designer Rabih Kayrouz (*see page 59*).
soukeltayeb.com/beit/beit-douma

Dar Alma, Tyre
Philippe Tabet's boutique hotel and restaurant is perched on a tiny beach next to the remains of a Crusader fortress.
daralmatyre.com

Eddésands Hotel & Wellness Resort, Byblos
A tropical seaside retreat with cabanas, a hotel, swimming pools and restaurants.
eddesands.com

Jammal, Kfar Abida
Set up in 1981 by Joe Jammal as a place to break bread with family and friends.
jammalrestaurant.com

Lazy B, Jieh
This environmentally conscious beach club offers guests access to man-made pools and natural creeks.
lazyb.me

Pierre and Friends, Thoum
This beach club is the ultimate day-to-night destination.
+961 (0)3 352 930

01 Picturesque village in the Chouf region
02 Local resident
03–04 Beit Douma guesthouse
05–06 Dar Alma hotel in Tyre
07–08 Roman ruins in Baalbeck

Resources
—— Inside knowledge

Now that you're confident enough to hail a cab and know where to take it, here's some additional advice to help you connect the dots. We begin with some more transport tips – you can never have enough automotive advice in a city as chaotic as this – and a few choice phrases to smooth out your transactions. Get into the swing of things with our Lebanese playlist and plan your trip around the best annual events in Beirut (and beyond). We've even included some suggestions for those days when the weather just isn't cooperating.

Transport
Getting around town

01 Getting around: The best way to get between Beirut's As and Bs is to hail a *servees* (shared taxi). Look out for their red number plates, flag one down and shout your destination; don't expect modern cars with mod cons. Alternatively, for a service that comes to you (complete with seatbelts) either use an app or call a reputable taxi firm such as Allo, Trust and White Taxi.

02 Getting out of town: To make it to the mountains, ask the above private taxi companies about their fares for longer journeys. If you're on a shoestring budget you can also hop on one of the minibuses, which operate in a similar way to servees taxis. Be warned, though: they get crowded and the drivers are notoriously reckless.

Airports
Runway success

Beirut Rafic Hariri International Airport sits about 8km south of the city centre and is the only airport that serves the Lebanese capital. Middle East Airlines offers direct flights from many major European and Middle Eastern cities and is the primary carrier to and from Beirut. The easiest way to get into town is via taxi but it's best to book ahead with one of the above private companies to avoid exorbitant markups at the taxi rank.

Vocabulary
Local lingo

In Lebanon a number of words and phrases are commonly spoken in English or French, including "hi" and "bonjour". If you want to try your hand at Arabic, however, this list will get you started.

01 Kifak (m)/kifik (f) How are you?
02 Shou fi ma fi? What's up? (literally "what's up, what's not up?")
03 Yeslamo: Thank you (literally "may your hands be protected")
04 Tekram ainak (m)/ ainik (f): You're welcome (literally "may your eye's desire be honoured")
05 Yalla: Come on/let's go
06 Khalas: Stop it/don't worry about it

Soundtrack to the city
Top tunes

01 Fairuz, 'Li Beirut': A bittersweet ode to Lebanese life that's loaded with feeling.
02 Mashrou' Leila, 'Tayf': This track by the alt-rock songsmiths is a hopeful and toe-tapping tale of resistance.
03 Scrambled Eggs, 'See You in Beirut': This band has been rattling the rafters for some 20 years with tracks like this.
04 Soap Kills, 'Aranis': Mixing traditional Arabic sounds with trip-hop beats, this track captures the joy of the Corniche.
05 Majida el Roumi, 'Ya Beirut': An uplifting paean to Lebanon's capital, courtesy of the country's best soprano.

Best events
What to see

01 Irtijal, citywide: The International Festival of Experimental Music. *April, irtijal.org*

02 Beirut Spring Festival, citywide: Theatre and music based on diversity. *June, beirutspringfestival.org*

03 Byblos International Festival, Byblos: Big name acts with an ocean backdrop. *July to August, byblosfestival.org*

04 Beiteddine Art Festival, Beiteddine: World music in a 200-year-old palace. *July to August, beiteddine.org*

05 Ehdeniyat International Festival, Ehden: Recreation in the mountain town of Ehden. *July to August, ehdeniyat.com*

06 Baalbeck International Festival, Baalbeck: The most prestigious cultural event in the region. *July to August, baalbeck.org.lb*

07 Beirut Art Fair, citywide: New artists, galleries and trends. *September, beirut-art-fair.com*

08 Beirut International Film Festival, citywide: Bringing a bold selection of arthouse films to Beirut. *October, beirutfilmfestival.org*

09 Beirut Art Film Festival, Sursock: Films on archaeology, opera et al. *November, bafflebanon.org*

10 Beirut & Beyond International Music Festival, citywide: Popular music from the Arab region and beyond. *December, beirutandbeyond.net*

Sunny days
The great outdoors

Stifling sun is a staple of the Beirut summer but thankfully there are ways to escape the exhaust fumes and unforgiving heat. Getting wet, getting out of town and getting high are all great options. Here are our tips.

01 Splash out: What better way to start a sunny day than with a revitalising jog around the traffic-free Corniche. Work up a sweat before cooling off in the pools at Sporting Club (*see page 122*), then hire a kayak or paddle board and get a closer look at Pigeon's Rock.

02 Wine and dine: Alternatively, escape the city altogether by heading to Chateau Ksara in the Bekaa Valley. Avoid the searing sunshine by going underground and enjoy a tour of the caves in which Ksara's finest vintages are stored. Naturally the tour concludes with a tasting session so you'll know exactly which bottle to pick up when you exit through the wineshop. *chateauksara.com*

03 Hit the roof: Back in the city, wind down your sunny day with a cocktail at Coop D'état. This hip rooftop hangout offers live music, great drinks and a place to watch the blistering sun slip away. Alternatively, head to the heart of Hamra and cool off at Pool D'état. Be sure to pack some swimwear and an appetite – this verdant rooftop bar sports a swimming pool and serves excellent salads. *saifigardens.com; hamragardens.com*

Rainy days
Weather-proof activities

In Beirut, when it rains it pours. Lebanon's Mediterranean climate can bring black clouds and rolling thunder to this coastal city so it's good to have a plan to hand when lightning strikes and the heavens open.

01 Wonders of the Sea Museum, Jdeideh: If the weather's too rough for you to experience the sea firsthand then head to this museum, where you can marvel at the wonders of the Med without getting wet. This museum hosts an array of maritime inhabitants – including eels, sponges and sharks – in a traditional Lebanese house just 10 minutes from the city centre. *wondersofthesea.net*

02 Musée de la Préhistoire Libanaise, Monot: Part of the Saint Joseph University, this museum focuses on the prehistory of the Arab Middle East. Discover the tools used by prehistoric man, alongside reconstructions of prehistoric weapons and spectacularly preserved fauna. *usj.edu.lb/mpl*

03 Banque Du Liban Museum, Hamra: Numismatists unite! Uncover the history of Lebanese currency at the Bank of Lebanon's museum. Alongside its rare historic coins and notes, video installations and games make for an enriching experience here. Entry is free too so you're sure to get your money's worth. *bdl.gov.lb*

About Monocle
─── Step inside

London HQ
───
Our editorial office is in Marylebone

In 2007, Monocle was launched as a monthly magazine briefing on global affairs, business, culture, design and much more. We believed there was a globally minded audience of readers who were hungry for opportunities and experiences beyond their national borders.

Today Monocle is a complete media brand with print, audio and online elements – not to mention our expanding network of shops and cafés. Besides our London HQ we have international bureaux in Toronto, Tokyo, Zürich and Hong Kong, with more on the way. We continue to grow and flourish and at our core is the simple belief that there will always be a place for a print brand that is committed to telling fresh stories and sending photographers on assignments. It's also a case of knowing that our success is all down to the readers, advertisers and collaborators who have supported us along the way.

1

International reach
Boots on the ground

We have a headquarters in London and call upon firsthand reports from our contributors in more than 35 cities around the world. For this travel guide, MONOCLE reporters Mikaela Aitken, Sean McGeady and Venetia Rainey decamped to Beirut to explore all that it has to offer. They also called on the assistance of contacts in the city to ensure that we have covered the best in retail, food and drink, hospitality, entertainment and more.

2

Online
Digital delivery

We have a dynamic website: *monocle.com*. As well as being the place to hear our radio station, Monocle 24, the site presents our films, which are beautifully shot and edited by our in-house team and provide a fresh perspective on our stories. Check out the films celebrating the cities that make up our Travel Guide Series before you explore the rest of the site.

3

Retail and cafés
Food for thought

Via our shops in Hong Kong, Toronto, Zürich, Tokyo and London we sell products that cater to our readers' tastes and are produced in collaboration with brands we believe in. We also have cafés in Tokyo, Zürich and London. And if you are in the UK capital visit the Kioskafé in Paddington, which combines good coffee and great reads.

4

Print
Committed to the page

MONOCLE is published 10 times a year. We also produce two standalone publications – THE FORECAST, packed with insights into the year ahead, and THE ESCAPIST, our summer travel-minded magazine – and seasonal weekly newspapers. Since 2013 we have also been publishing books, like this one, in partnership with Gestalten. Visit *monocle.com/subscribe*.

5

Radio
Sound approach

Monocle 24 is our round-the-clock radio station that was launched in 2011. It delivers global news and shows covering foreign affairs, urbanism, business, culture, food and drink, design and print media. When you find yourself in Beirut, tune into *The Globalist* in the morning for a newsy start to your day. You can listen live or download our shows from *monocle.com*, iTunes or SoundCloud.

Priority service
——
Subscribers save 10 per cent in our online shop

Join the club

01
Subscribe to Monocle
A subscription is a simple way to make sure that you never miss an issue – and you'll enjoy many additional benefits.

02
Be in the know
Our subscribers have exclusive access to the entire Monocle archive, and priority access to selected product collaborations, at *monocle.com*.

03
Stay in the loop
Subscription copies are delivered to your door at no extra cost no matter where you are in the world. We also offer an auto-renewal service to ensure that you never miss an issue.

04
And there's more…
Subscribers benefit from a 10 per cent discount at all Monocle shops, including online, and receive exclusive offers and invitations to events around the world.

Choose your package

Premium one year
12 × issues
+ Porter Sub Club bag

One year
12 × issues
+ Monocle Voyage tote bag

Six months
6 × issues

Chief photographer
Anna Maria Nielsen

Still life
David Sykes

Photographers
Alex Atack
Felix Brüggemanni
James Haines-Young
Natalie Naccache
Felix Odell
Tanya Traboulsi

Images
Diane Aftimos
GdeLaubier
Rami Haj
Jörg Koopman
Noël Nasr
Marco Pinarelli

Illustrators
Satoshi Hashimoto
Ceylan Sahin
Tokuma

Writers
Mikaela Aitken
Nasri Atallah
Carole Corm
Nolan Giles
Sophie Grove
Bahi Ghubril
Tala Hajjar
Giles Khoury
Tomos Lewis
Christopher Lord
Sean McGeady
Sally Moussawi
Kamal Mouzawak
Venetia Rainey
Alex Rowell
Katie Watkins

Monocle
EDITOR IN CHIEF AND
CHAIRMAN
Tyler Brûlé
EDITOR
Andrew Tuck
CREATIVE DIRECTOR
Richard Spencer Powell

Beirut
Acknowledgements

Need to know
Mikaela Aitken

H **1**
Hotels
Mikaela Aitken

F **2**
Food and drink
Venetia Rainey

R **3**
Retail
Mikaela Aitken

T **4**
Things we'd buy
Mikaela Aitken

E **5**
Essays
Mikaela Aitken

C **6**
Culture
Sean McGeady

D **7**
Design and architecture
Venetia Rainey

S **8**
Sport and fitness
Mikaela Aitken

W **9**
Walks
Mikaela Aitken

O **10**
Out of town
Mikaela Aitken

Resources
Sean McGeady

**The Monocle Travel Guide
Series: Beirut**
GUIDE EDITOR
Mikaela Aitken
ASSOCIATE GUIDE EDITORS
Sean McGeady
Venetia Rainey
PHOTO EDITOR
Victoria Cagol

**The Monocle Travel Guide
Series**
SERIES EDITOR
Joe Pickard
ASSOCIATE EDITOR
Chloë Ashby
ASSISTANT EDITOR
Mikaela Aitken
WRITER
Melkon Charchoglyan
DESIGNER
Loi Xuan Ly
PHOTO EDITORS
Matthew Beaman
Victoria Cagol
Shin Miura

PRODUCTION
Jacqueline Deacon
Dan Poole
Rachel Kurzfield
Sean McGeady
Sonia Zhuravlyova

Research
Beatrice Carmi
Melkon Charchoglyan
Dan Einav
Audrey Fiodorenko
Leiah Fournier
Will Kitchens
Tom Melville
Hester Underhill

Special thanks
Mohamad Abdouni
Louise Banbury
David Corm
Hiram Corm
Firas Abou Fakher
Elie Harfouche
Mira Hawa
Krikor Jabotian
Abdul-Halim Jabr
Muriel Kahwagi
Pete Kempshall
Jana Momtaz
Rouba Mourtada
Samir Moussawi
Rana Salam

The MONOCLE *Travel Guide Series* 26 ◉
San Francisco

The MONOCLE *Travel Guide Series* 27 ◉
Kyoto

New

The collection
Planning another trip? We have a global suite of guides, with many more set to be released in the coming months. Cities are fun. Let's explore.

The MONOCLE *Travel Guide Series* 28 ◉
Seoul

The MONOCLE *Travel Guide Series* 29 ◉
Barcelona

◉
Buy today at all good bookshops
───
You can also visit the online shops at *monocle.com* and *shop.gestalten.com* to get hold of your copies.

Right, where next?